CW00957014

Management – Skills a

Roger Oldcorn is an industrial ⟨…⟩
Management College – where he is Deputy ⟨…⟩
Management Development and Advisory Service. He worked in the
food and hotel industries for several years before joining the Centre
for Interfirm Comparison, where he was Senior Projects Manager.
He has carried out long-term assignments for the United Nations
(UNIDO) in India and the Middle East and also worked as a
consultant in the USA. He has been in management education since
the mid-1970s and was Business Development Advisor at Kingston
Regional Management Centre before moving to Henley. His
particular interests include the economic, financial and accounting
aspects of corporate planning and business development.

Roger Oldcorn is the author of *Management: A Fresh Approach* and
Understanding Company Accounts in the Pan Breakthrough series; he
is the author of *Company Accounts* and *The Management of Business* in
the Pan Management Guides series.

PAN MANAGEMENT GUIDES
Other books in the series:

PAN MANAGEMENT GUIDES

Management – Skills and Functions

Roger Oldcorn

A Pan Original
Pan Books London, Sydney and Auckland

First published 1988 by Pan Books Ltd,
Cavaye Place, London sw10 9pg
9 8 7 6 5 4 3 2 1
© Roger Oldcorn 1988
ISBN 0 330 29968 9
Photoset by Rowland Phototypesetting Ltd,
Bury St Edmunds, Suffolk
Printed and bound in Great Britain
by Cox and Wyman Ltd, Reading, Berks.

This book is sold subject to the condition that it
shall not, by way of trade or otherwise, be lent, re-sold,
hired out, or otherwise circulated without the publisher's prior
consent in any form of binding or cover other than that in which
it is published and without a similar condition including this
condition being imposed on the subsequent purchaser

Acknowledgements

This book could not have been written without the help and support of many people. In particular I should like to thank the following: Steven Mair, formerly Editorial Director of Management and Business Books, at Pan Books, who encouraged me to write and who kept the good ideas flowing; Professor John Adair, whose books on leadership and on decision-making are invaluable sources of wisdom and with whom discussion is so stimulating; Ian Hinton at Kingston Regional Management Centre for his wise counsel, his deep knowledge of all things managerial and his unfailing good spirits; Jane Cranwell-Ward at Henley, for much advice, for teaching me about managing stress and freely answering all my questions on motivation; Loraine Isherwood, who averted a crisis by producing decent typescript when the deadline was much too close for comfort. Most important of all, a very special thank you goes to my wife Dorothy, who not only successfully manages a job, a home and a family, but me too.

For
my Mother

Introduction

People have been managing things for thousands of years; you only need to look at the Pyramids to appreciate that they did not appear by magic or by wishful thinking, but because some managers got things planned and organized and then set about turning those dreams into reality.

Most managers are not in the position to take part in a project as exciting as Pyramid construction, yet many things are happening these days which are interesting and, to a degree, exciting. The excitement comes partly from living in an age when we cannot be sure what tomorrow will bring. For example, a company I know existed happily for years as the UK subsidiary of an American corporation, turning in good profits year by year. Then one day, out of the blue, the parent company decided to float off the UK part as an independent publicly quoted company.

To use the word 'traumatic' is not out of place in this situation. Managers had to learn new skills overnight, carry the rest of the staff along and shoulder the burden of responsibility for getting the new status of the firm established on time, as well as keeping the business going. It was incredibly hard and stressful work, but in the end a most rewarding experience.

Good management is about creating opportunities for the organization and making sure that these opportunities are realized as efficiently and effectively as possible. As Chester Barnard wrote many years ago, the executive task is not only to decide the purpose of the organization, but also to 'secure the essential effort' needed for its achievement. My aim in this book is to identify the skills and functions that are necessary for managers to be able to secure that essential effort, and to describe the ways in which the managerial task can be accomplished efficiently.

The book is intended for the new manager, or for anyone aspiring to a job at a managerial level, and is offered in the hope that as a result of reading it, they will be encouraged to set about improving the effectiveness and efficiency of the department, function or business for which they are responsible.

The managers who built the Pyramids did not attend a business school or management college – so far as we know – nor was there much in the way of textbooks on management. If they could be so successful without all these aids, think how much more successful today's managers can be if all the lessons and experience can be harnessed. There is plenty of good management practice to be found nowadays, yet there are still areas of inefficiency in all walks of life, where the managers are labelled incompetent. These managers often assume they have no need of management training; that assumption needs to be challenged forcefully, because all managers can develop their skills – there is always room for improvement.

Contents

1 What is Management?

The job of management can cover many different tasks and functions, and numerous attempts have been made to classify and describe them. Yet underlying them all, as we will see, is the idea that management is concerned with taking responsibility. In this respect, responsibility means handling matters of wider importance than those which are merely personal and domestic. Moreover, the range of concerns to be managed these days is vast: from supermarkets and football clubs to hospitals, factories, offices and schools. Whoever is responsible for the affairs of all these organizations – in part or in whole – is a manager.

To gain some idea of the scope of the tasks and functions of management nowadays, take a quick look at the 'jobs pages' in the papers. It very quickly becomes apparent that there are two kinds of requirement for a managerial job.

In the first place there are technical and professional needs: a computer manager needs to know about computers, a car sales manager requires selling skills and a knowledge of motor cars, the manager of a scientific laboratory must be knowledgeable about the branch of science being researched, and the football club manager has to know a great deal about soccer.

The second kind of requirement in a managerial job bears no relationship to the trade or profession to be managed. In fact the same words crop up time and again, irrespective of the organization and its sector of the economy. Common words and phrases in the job advertisements include:

- *motivate and lead a team of . . .*
- *develop and control a major project*
- *establish plans*
- *must be numerate*
- *. . . excellent inter-personal and man-management skills*
- *lead through a period of rapid change*

■ *first-class communicator*
■ *formulate policies*

As well as all these, there are additional requirements such as being 'energetic', 'creative' and 'possessing business acumen'.

The functions of management

There are a number of ways to classify these managerial skills and functions, and one of the best-known was developed by the French businessman Henri Fayol back in 1916.

Fayol took an ailing coal-mine and turned it into a successful business in coal and steel. His book *General and Industrial Management* identifies five elements or functions of management. They are:

■ *Planning*
■ *Organizing*
■ *Command*
■ *Coordination*
■ *Control*

It is worth considering in more detail exactly what Fayol meant by these five words:

■ *Planning* is looking ahead and preparing for the future. The key word is 'foresight', which means both making an assessment of the future and actually doing something about it. Fayol was keen on the technique of forecasting and considered that failure to plan signifies managerial incompetence.
■ *Organizing* is providing the business with everything it needs to operate efficiently (equipment, materials, finance, people).
■ *Command* is getting things done by subordinates. The word itself may not be too appealing: it suggests the Army and being ordered about. Remember that the book was written at the time of the First World War, when the style was 'giving and receiving orders'. However, Fayol did not use the word in this narrow sense but rather in terms of making sure that

things get done, the words 'direct' and 'leadership' being
important alternatives.
■ *Coordination* is the task of harmonizing all the elements and
activities to ensure that everything is in the right place at the
right time and in the right amounts.
■ *Control* is making sure that events turn out the way they are
planned.

These days it is usual to consider the management functions as
threefold:
   PLANNING – which includes organizing and coordination
   COMMAND – which embraces leadership and motivating
staff
   CONTROL

Managerial qualities

As well as the five functions of management, Fayol described six
groups of qualities which managers should possess:

■ *physical:* healthy and vigorous
■ *mental:* able to learn and to adapt; judgement; mental vigour
■ *moral:* firmness; acceptance of responsibility; initiative; loyalty;
  tact
■ *education:* good general education
■ *special knowledge:* for the work
■ *experience*

Scientific management

Around the same period as Henri Fayol's work, the American,
F. W. Taylor, wrote his book *The Principles of Scientific Management*
which showed a marked contrast to Fayol's ideas and has formed
the basis of much management thinking since. He is now known
as the father of scientific management, which is often (mis-
takenly) thought to be exclusively concerned with 'time and
motion study' and stop-watches.

Taylor was concerned about inefficiency and asserted that the cure was systematic management. He became chief engineer in the Midvale Steel Company in Philadelphia in 1884 and was troubled by the waste of human effort in the steel-making process. He sought out the best way of doing things, using a scientific approach to work, he stressed such aspects as planning and training and made it clear that management must take responsibility for its actions.

Functions of the Executive

One of the most important of the early thinkers on management was Chester Barnard, who was president of the New Jersey Bell Telephone Company from 1927 to 1952. He saw the task of the manager (or executive) as being to determine the purpose of the organization and to develop an effective system of communications so that that purpose could be achieved. He emphasized that executives need many skills in order to be really effective; decision-making skills and intelligence being most important.

What do managers do?

In the last twenty years a considerable amount of research has been undertaken to try to answer this question. One famous piece of work in Britain was conducted by Rosemary Stewart, who asked: 'How do the managers spend their time?' The answers to this question produced five categories of manager:

- *emissaries* – they spend much time away from the organization, dealing with suppliers, customers, banks and so on.
- *talkers* – those who spend a great deal of their time having discussions with others.
- *writers* – including reading and calculating.
- *trouble-shooters* – who sort out problems and crises and whose work is fragmented. These managers spend much time with subordinates.

■ *committee men* – who are often involved in group discussions.

Another interesting piece of research was carried out by Henry Mintzberg in the USA. He identifies ten managerial roles which can be divided into three categories:

interpersonal roles
■ figurehead (largely ceremonial duties)
■ leader
■ liaison (with others within and outside the organization)
informational roles
■ monitor (assessing information)
■ disseminator
■ spokesman
decision-making roles
■ entrepreneur
■ disturbance handler (managing change)
■ resource allocator
■ negotiator

These studies by Stewart and Mintzberg are important because they show clearly the wide range of activities which managers are called upon to perform. Indeed, if we look at any managerial job, it becomes apparent that to carry out this wide range of activities effectively, an equally wide range of skills, knowledge and abilities is needed:

■ *Knowledge* – of the trade, profession or vocation; the organization; the industry and its environment.
■ *Skills* – relating to solving problems, taking decisions, communicating, leading, motivating, handling people, managing change.
■ *Ability* – to plan, control, organize.

Today's effective manager

It is a useful exercise to consider any really effective managers you know. Which of all the above factors does that individual possess? Equally, if you know any really poor managers, the list is useful in enabling you to identify *why* they are so poor. It should be readily apparent that the best managers are those who try continually to improve their knowledge, skills and ability. One thing is certain: those people who are really effective in managing others also manage themselves effectively.

In the chapters that follow, I will be examining these skills and abilities in order to identify what counts as good practice, not only in the real world of management but also in the literature on the subject.

2 Planning and Control

Your first task as a manager is to ensure that the activities for which you are responsible are successful, which demands a good deal of thinking about the future and also taking action well in advance to make sure that all goes well. This is what planning is all about. Equally important, however, is the function of control which is concerned with ensuring that what you have planned is what actually takes place.

Levels of planning

Generally, three levels of planning can be identified.

Operational planning or tactical planning is the most common. This is carried out at all managerial levels in the organization, relates to the immediate future (often the following year) and is described in some detail.

Project planning is carried out for special activities. Construction firms prepare project plans for every job they undertake, whether it is building a house or the Channel Tunnel.

Strategic planning is concerned with the long-term future of the organization. Sometimes this is referred to as long-range planning because the 'planning horizon' lies many years in the future. Any company where there is a lengthy time-lag between deciding on a course of action and the event itself, is familiar with strategic planning. Oil companies, the aircraft industry, motor manufacture – all need strategic planning: that is obvious. However, it should be a normal feature in all organizations whatever their business, as any company that is not thinking strategically, may well find itself unable to compete effectively in the future.

Aims and objectives

A useful starting point for any planning exercise is to ask the question: What are we trying to achieve? The answer may be very personal in the case of a small firm, such as, 'I want to make a fortune and retire to the Bahamas when I reach the age of 60.' In contrast, the declared aim of many big corporations is to satisfy the shareholders in the long run.

In the public sector, aims will include statements such as 'to provide an efficient service, at reasonable cost'; this kind of statement will also appear at the level of a department or function within an organization. Hopefully the word 'efficient' will be defined to include the speed and scope of the service.

Where a project is being planned, the importance of clear aims and objectives is critical. A vague statement such as 'We aim to build a house' is of very little use without the other key details such as where, how big and the completion date.

Definitions

Aims   Usually general statements about the organization's ambitions, which may include a statement about its underlying purpose or *mission*.
Objectives   The precise things being aimed at, including the element of time.
Targets   The specific numbers being aimed at.

The manager's aims checklist

You should set out the aims and objectives of the activities for which you are responsible. To do so, ask yourself:

- What is the mission of the organization and the underlying purpose of the activity?
- What is the activity aiming to achieve?
- What specific objectives need to be set?
- What time-scale is envisaged?
- What are the targets in measurable terms?

Forecasting

Henri Fayol was very keen that managers should make forecasts as part of the planning process. Forecasting is no more than an estimate of what is likely to happen at a specific time in the future. Inside an organization the forecast assumes that we will continue to operate in the way we are doing now, while an external forecast makes some assumptions about trends in the environment of the organization.

You can see the importance of a forecast in planning from this simple example:

The planning department of a New Town was able to process twenty planning applications a week. It was forecast that the population of the town would double in five years, with twice as many houses and almost double the number of companies. It was obvious that either the department would become much less efficient or else more staff should be employed. Since it takes over a year to get a new member of staff fully trained, a recruitment drive over the period was essential.

Getting the facts

This stage in the planning process is often called a SWOT analysis, the letters standing for:

- *Strengths*
- *Weaknesses*
- *Opportunities*
- *Threats*

Effective planning depends on identifying these factors as precisely as you can because:

- strengths are to be built on;
- weaknesses are to be cured (or avoided);
- opportunities are to be grasped; and
- threats are to be avoided (or removed).

Evaluating strengths and weaknesses

People In all organizations the most important asset is people. A regular and systematic review of their strengths and weaknesses should be conducted in order to identify such things as the age structure of the staff (are there too many old people and insufficient new blood?), their skills (are they qualified to take on new responsibilities? How well trained are they?), and how well motivated they are.

Products and services The important questions to ask are: is there sufficient demand for our products or services? and are they likely to go on being in demand in the future? These questions are relevant within a department or function as well as for the organization as a whole. For example, a large firm may have a fleet of vehicles to deliver its products. However, if the distribution function is inefficient, the firm may decide to disband the fleet and use a general haulage company instead.

Finance For most managers the main financial problem is whether their budget for the forthcoming year is adequate and whether they will be able to spend money on capital items. But behind these problems lie questions about the organization's overall financial health and (in the private sector) its profitability. Clearly, an organization with a cash shortage will be unable to grow and develop.

Physical resources Under this heading the two important items to evaluate are space and equipment. A firm working in cramped, old buildings is at a disadvantage; so too is an organization with out-of-date or insufficient equipment – the office typewriter being the most common example. Poor physical resources can lead to inefficiency and a lack of motivation and will hamper the organization's prospects.

The organization The important questions you should ask in relation to this are:
   Is the structure sensible in that lines of communication are to be short and that responsibilities are clearly established?
   Are the systems time-wasting or useful?

Management No evaluation is complete without considering the managers. Are they skilled and experienced? Are they capable of taking on greater responsibilities? Are they providing leadership? Are they forward-looking?

Opportunities and threats

All organizations are influenced and affected by their environments and all managers need to be aware of the elements of the outside world which are likely to provide opportunities or pose threats. It is convenient to split these elements into six:

- Economic
- Technological and scientific
- Political and legal
- Social
- Competitive (for business firms)
- Natural

Economic factors It is important for you to have a view on:

- the predicted growth of the economy in the sectors and regions where your organization operates;
- inflation;
- interest rates (especially if you want to borrow money);
- the way your currency may fluctuate against the currency of countries you deal with.

Technological and scientific factors The important questions to ask are: Is the science and technology that we use likely to improve or change significantly in the near future? Are our products likely to be out of date soon? Is the competition likely to get ahead of us technologically?

Political and legal factors In this category the question to ask is: Are there likely to be any new laws (locally, nationally or internationally) which will make things easier or more difficult for us? Any such laws may relate to health and safety at work, how companies operate, employment of staff, or they may be regulations affecting trading itself, such as importing.

Social factors Social trends are important aspects of the environment for many organizations. Some trends are classified as 'fashion' – popular today, but not next year. Others are 'seven-day wonders' – like skateboards. Yet others involve a gradual change over the years, such as the trends away from smoking and away from the cinema.

Competitive factors For all business organizations, competition is often seen as the most dangerous threat. A direct competitor has to be watched, as has the indirect competitor – the firm selling similar (though not identical) services or products. Firms should also be aware of potential competition. If the existing market does not have much competition and is profitable, then sooner or later some firm or other will try to break in – as the motor-cycle industry in Britain discovered.

Natural factors The main factors under this heading are *population* and *climate*. The important aspects of population for you to consider are movement to or from a particular region; changes in the class of people living in an area, and whether the age profile of the population is changing. Climate is important if you are a farmer, play cricket or run a brewery. Forecasting climatic change is notoriously difficult, but if the worst is expected then at least you can set up contingency plans to offset the worst effects.

Evaluation of environmental factors is most obviously carried out at the level of the organization as a whole. However, in their own planning process departmental managers should also take note of those factors outside their control which affect departmental performance. It is always good thinking to realistically identify what might happen in the environment to upset the status quo.

Strategy formulation

Strategy is a statement of the way in which objectives are going to be met, and there are four fundamental strategic options that business organizations can adopt:

- *Improve current operations*
- *Expand the markets served*
- *Extend the range of products or services offered*
- *Diversify*

Improvement

Improvement as a strategy implies trying to be more efficient at your current line of business. It assumes that, within the organization, there are weaknesses that can be overcome; also that the markets currently being served could yield more business. Sometimes a very weak firm may have no other option than to be more efficient, especially if there is a cash shortage. Similarly, departmental managers may have no other choice than to focus on efficiency and productivity improvements.

Expand markets

A relatively easy way to extend a business activity is to offer the firm's goods or services in markets which have not previously been tapped. The large supermarket chains are growing in this way, and exporting is a logical step for a manufacturer who is covering the home market thoroughly.

Extend product range

In this strategy, additional products or services are offered in the existing markets. With many products this will involve considerable research and development expenditure and is considered fairly risky, since there is no guarantee that the new offering will be accepted by the market. Countless numbers of new products and services launched each year are very quickly abandoned, but those which do succeed pay handsome dividends.

Inside an organization, a successful departmental strategy is to offer additional services to other departments within one's area of expertise. This has the effect of expanding the department and also its status within the organization.

Diversify

This is the most risky strategy of all, because it involves developing new products or services and offering them in new markets. In both aspects the firm has no direct experience and so is taking a leap into the unknown. Obviously, if the new product or service and the new market are similar to the old, then there is a better chance of success. Similarly, buying an existing firm which is successful in the new activity has a better chance of success than if the idea is home-grown. Even so, diversification is risky and doing something totally different is riskiest of all. This is known as conglomerate diversification and there are only a few diversified firms which are very successful.

Operational planning

All managers should be involved in operational planning. Once objectives have been set and a broad strategy determined, your next task as manager is to work out in detail what needs to be done; this is operational or tactical planning. Usually, the time frame of such plans is quite short – a year or two is normal – and they should contain statements on every aspect of the operation which is of any importance. Certainly it must be clear from the operational plans what the key tasks are, who is responsible for carrying them out and when they should be accomplished. Good plans often have further contingency plans built in, so that if things do go wrong a disaster can be avoided – which is why, in the theatre, every actor has an understudy.

The outcome of a good planning activity should be the budget. This is no more than a statement of plans in financial terms, but its construction should enable everyone to see whether the plans are realistic from the monetary viewpoint: whether they require too much money, and also whether they will generate enough money.

Project planning

Projects can range from building a nuclear-powered electricity works to staging a rock concert, running an advertising campaign or decorating the kitchen. The principles are the same and correspond with those of strategic and tactical planning too. The important difference with a project is that there is a specific end in sight – namely, completion.

Two factors which are critical in all projects are time and money. The job has to be finished within a specified budget and by a specified date, and it often seems that the bigger the project the greater the potential for delay and overspending.

In good project planning you must:

- decide what resources are needed at each stage (materials, equipment, people, money)
- determine when each stage must be completed
- secure the agreement of everyone involved that the time and money estimates are viable.

Five rules for good planning

1 Allow plenty of time.
2 Involve all managers.
3 Leave nothing to chance.
4 Quantify (budgets, etc.).
5 Set milestones (intermediate stages when certain things have to be achieved).

Control

Control essentially means making sure that things turn out in the way we intended. To control a ship means to steer it in such a way that we end up at the projected destination and not on the rocks. Similarly, as a manager you must ensure that your area of responsibility achieves the aims and objectives set out for it; you must keep things under control. In other words, effective control makes successful planning.

Good control systems contain several key elements:

■ *Make a plan*

This must be set out in measurable terms because it is difficult to control anything unless there is a yardstick for comparison. To control a central-heating system, an ideal temperature is needed. To control money, a budget is required. To control the amount of fuel used by a car or lorry, a miles-per-gallon or per-litre figure is needed. All these are plans in numerical terms; sometimes they are called budgets, sometimes standards and sometimes formulae, recipes or specifications.

■ *Compare*

This stage is sometimes called monitoring – which simply means checking up on what is going on – and is carried out by comparing actual performance with the plan. To check that the quantity of goods being delivered to me corresponded with what I ordered, I would count the actual amount delivered and compare that with the order. If the pilot of an aeroplane wants to be sure of arriving at the planned destination, he continually monitors his direction: he compares the actual with the course plotted at the start.

You should make frequent comparisons; the more important the item to be controlled, the more frequent must be the comparison.

■ *Assess the difference*

If what is actually happening tallies exactly with what was planned, then there is no problem and all is under control. However, if there is a difference then there may be a problem. For example, suppose that the cost of a particular item over a month was budgeted at £50,000 and we discovered that the actual cost was £60,000. Is there a problem or not? As always, the answer depends on the circumstances. If the total departmental budget was only £70,000, then an increase in actual expenditure of £10,000 would be very significant. If, however, the context of the item was an overall budget of tens of millions of pounds, we may choose to ignore it.

The key word is 'significant'; there is only a problem if there is a significant variance between planned and actual.

■ *Communicate*

If the variance is significant, then it is important that this information is passed on to the people who can do something about it. Nothing will be done unless someone with power and authority is notified. On the other hand, it is also important to pass on the news when things are going according to plan. This is one aspect of the manager's job which is often overlooked: when things are going well, people appreciate being informed of the fact, as we will see when we look at motivation (Chapter 5).

■ *Take action*

There is no point in having a clever reporting system if nothing happens. If you are the manager who is responsible, then you must take action if there is a significant variance, because if you do nothing the situation rapidly gets totally out of hand. At sea, a slight deviation from the set course can be corrected with a touch on the tiller, but if nothing is done, the deviation becomes a major change in the route which could put the ship on the rocks. At work, neglect a minor fault and very soon it becomes a major problem.

There are three possible courses of action to take when a variance has been found:

—*do nothing* If you are fairly certain that the variance was a one-off freak occurrence and will have no significant effect on the way things eventually turn out, then to do nothing is reasonable; but this has to be a positive decision.

—*take corrective action* If things are not operating according to plan – and you are sure the plans are reasonable – then find out what caused actual events to differ from them and act accordingly.

—*change the plan* It could be that events outside your control have made the plans themselves meaningless. For example, a sudden increase in the price of petrol would cause an adverse variance in the fuel costs of a taxi. In this case a revision of the plan is needed so as to account for the higher cost of fuel and also to find a way of offsetting its effects by making savings elsewhere.

■ *Be quick*

Speedy communications are needed at all stages of a control system so that the moment a variance occurs, action can be taken. There is not much merit in a system which reports in April that a fall of 20% in sales occurred in January. Ideally the information should be made known before the end of the month, and action taken so that the problem is not repeated in February.

■ *Count the cost*

Good control systems cost money to set up and run. Sometimes this cost is out of proportion to the potential losses which might occur if there was no system. Thus it would be pointless to have a system costing £20,000 a year for controlling the use of paper-clips when the total annual cost of the function was only £450. On the other hand, it is worth spending heavily on control systems where health and safety are at risk, where the potential losses are high or where the products being made are very expensive or of high quality.

Useful control systems

Budgetary control This is possibly the most common system in use. The budget is the plan in monetary terms, and the control system compares all actual expenditure and income against the appropriate budget. Major items are monitored weekly and most other items monthly. In addition to all the features described above, budgetary control needs:

■ the agreement of everyone involved
■ early preparation
■ everyone to understand the system
■ top management support
■ a degree of flexibility

Quality control Quality relates to all aspects of working life, not just products that are manufactured. In an hotel, quality is important in terms of cleanliness and service generally. In an office, quality refers to accurate work which is completed promptly and in a presentable manner. In all organizations these aspects of quality need to be controlled, otherwise standards begin to slip.

Stock control Wherever goods are stored, a system is needed to safeguard them from damage or theft. If the goods are perishable, of high value or can be easily sold, then more money will have to be spent on control.

Planning and control go together. It is not possible to have effective planning without good controls, since even the best-laid plans can go adrift. Moreover, to have a control system without a plan is impossible. Managers have responsibility in both areas, although in general the more junior you are as a manager the more time you will spend on actual control, while the more senior you become, so the amount of time spent on the planning process itself should increase. If this is not the case, then it is arguable that you are not doing your job properly.

3 Organizing

Organizing can be defined as the process of getting things done in the best and most efficient way. In a business which is entirely operated by one person, all the tasks are carried out by that individual, who knows what is going on in every part of the business. This ensures that there is no conflict between activities. In contrast, organizations employing more than one person need to create structures which enable the task to be carried out efficiently, so that work can be divided up sensibly.

Unfortunately, organizations do not stand still; they are continually changing and it is a well-known phenomenon that no sooner has a reorganization taken place, than the situation changes and the structure is no longer appropriate. What needs to be set up is an organization structure which is capable of being modified to fit new situations without massive upheaval; here there are a number of useful principles which can help.

Specialization

The need to employ specialists becomes obvious when looking at a small, young business. It is unlikely that the owner will have all the skills required to run the firm successfully, and in particular he may not have the necessary legal or financial skills. So initially he will employ the services of professional accountants and solicitors on a consultancy basis. Apart from these aspects, however, the owner of a very small firm has to be a good all-rounder.

As a small business grows, so assistants are employed to help the owner. In a shop this is a sales assistant, a plumber takes on a 'mate', while a part-time book-keeper is often employed to look after the money side of the concern.

Growth of the business is just one reason for staff being taken on in a small firm. The owner may decide that he should specialize in his own area of expertise – or on the aspects he enjoys (which can be dangerous if this detracts from the important jobs). He may not have sufficient skills himself, or he may find a particular job boring.

Similarly there are several good reasons for not taking on staff, including the obvious point that nobody hires assistance if there is a shortage of money. Moreover, some owners of small firms prefer not to have responsibility for staff in any way, favouring a complete do-it-yourself approach. This in turn can come about for several reasons, such as difficulty in getting on with people, unwillingness to become involved in all the legal matters that are required when others are employed, and also a fear of delegating work to someone else or an inability to do so.

Limits to specialization

Many managers would like to have a whole array of specialists working for them, so that they can get on with the 'really important' work. However, there are problems: as we noted above, money is a primary limiting factor, but there is also a motivating difficulty in that a narrow specialist may feel cut off from the main activities of the organization. This has been recognized in large-scale manufacturing industry, where carrying out a specific task of a specialized nature is necessary for high productivity. (This topic will be reviewed in Chapter 5 on Motivation.)

A further problem with specialization is that if there are a large number of experts, each operating in a very narrow area, communications, coordination and control become more difficult.

Delegation

Delegation is the process of passing out work to someone else; the moment a business hires its first employee, delegation is taking place. With simple routine tasks, delegation is relatively easy, while even the appointment of experts is not difficult so long as you follow three important rules:

- Train the staff until they are totally capable in the task
- Make sure the task is fully understood
- Set up clear lines of communication so they know who they report to, and ideally, arrange that everyone should report to only one other person.

Management delegation

The art of successful delegation is best seen at the managerial level, which can be illustrated if we consider the example of a small, growing retail business.

A shop will grow to a certain size where the owner is in charge of maybe some fifteen to twenty staff. If it is successful, the owner may decide to open another shop, say 10 miles away in the next town. The question he has to face is: How is he going to manage both shops? There are various choices.

He can continue to manage both himself by driving to and fro, keeping an eye on things all the time. There would be an office in or near one of the shops, but the problem with this arrangement is: who would handle all the telephone inquiries and deal with the suppliers' sales representatives?

To overcome the weaknesses of this set-up, most small firms will take the critical step of appointing a manager – either to one of the new shops, or to both shops. Appointing a manager for the first time is not an easy decision, because in so doing the owner feels he is giving away some of his personal power; he is trusting someone else with the business he has built up and he is, in effect, cutting himself off from the action and possibly from some old friends. Moreover – and this applies to all delegation – there is a feeling that nobody can do the job as well as you can yourself.

Managerial delegation has to be done, because there is no way of keeping track of everything that is going on in the organization. The owner's effective span of control is fifteen people on one site, not thirty people on two sites. In fact, the better choice would be to appoint a manager to be in charge of each shop. However, here is a practical difficulty: who is to be appointed as manager at each location? The future success of the firm may well hang on these appointments, so it is important to get it right. Possibly the best solution here would be to promote two of the existing staff to take up the new managerial positions. This would have the considerable advantage that they would know the owner, his values and attitudes, and there would be no settling-in period. Nevertheless, achieving this very desirable state of affairs requires considerable foresight.

Management delegation is, therefore, an inevitable step and involves handing over both authority and decision-making power. This is not easy for the owner and could be dangerous: it is hard because, as we have seen, he is cutting himself off; it is dangerous because he has to trust the manager to do the job properly.

Dividing the organization

The example described above relates to a decision to open a second branch of an organization in a new location. A shop was used for this example, but it could just as well be any type of activity where a split is needed. Dividing up an organization is often called 'departmentation', which simply means dividing into departments. There are many ways of doing this, and it is worth considering some of the main methods (this list also applies to the problem of dividing up work between individuals).

Geographically This is the way we have just considered and is obviously useful when it is important to be physically close to the territory in which your organization wants to operate. Moreover, local conditions may differ and the group responsible for looking after specific areas will build up expert knowledge of these. Rather than trying to do everything from head office, many firms will divide up the sales function (and later the production function), placing a separate function in each country or cluster of countries.

By function In manufacturing organizations the main functions are production and sales. In small firms, it is not uncommon that the first manager to be appointed by the owners is either a sales

manager or a manager in charge of 'operations'. As the organization grows, so the number of functional managers increases,
although some curious anomalies crop up such as the personnel
function being carried out by the chief accountant.

By product As organizations grow, the range of products or
services offered grows also. At first all the products are handled
by using common facilities, but there comes a time when the
volume being dealt with is so great that it is more advantageous to
treat each product or service as a separate company.

By customer This is particularly common in the selling function,
where it is felt that different customers require different treat-
ment.

By process Many operations, both clerical and in manufacturing,
are performed in sequence, and it is one of the features of modern
organizations that the sequences have tended to be split into
smaller and smaller parts. The reason for this is that each separate
process requires special skills; by specializing in a limited range of
work, the operator becomes highly efficient and thus raises his
productivity.

I have already noted the limitations of such specialization, and
to pursue this kind of departmentation to its logical conclusion
would result in all kinds of absurdities. Imagine what would
happen if the job of bus driver was divided up into five activities:
someone to start the vehicle, someone to drive it out of the
garage, another to drive it on the road, a fourth to put it back into
the garage and a fifth to stop the engine. The absurdity arises
because the system is inefficient and because each individual's
job is so narrow as to be very frustrating. This will be examined
again when we study the subject of motivation.

By numbers This system is used in, for instance, the Army and in
other situations where many people are needed to carry out very
similar tasks.

Alphabetically A common way of dividing up work which is all of a
similar nature is to do so on an alphabetical basis. This is normal
practice in offices where large volumes of similar material have to
be processed. One department will deal with all customers whose

surnames begin with the letters A, B or C; another department handles D, E and F and so on.

Which sort of division to choose

You must recognize that each method of dividing up an organization has its advantages and disadvantages. Some methods are obviously unsuitable: for instance, to divide up the management of British Rail alphabetically by name of station would be pointless! The key questions you should ask include:

- Does the division tie in with overall strategies?
- Does it cost more than any other method?
- How easy will it be to coordinate the separate parts?
- Could it lead to interdepartmental feuds? (Not avoidable in any split-up, but some are more likely to result in conflict than others.)
- Are the members of the team likely to be motivated by the arrangement or not?

How many subordinates?

On p. 24 we introduced the phrase 'span of control' with reference to the number of people working directly for the owner of a small shop. The expression has been in management literature for a long time, although a more apt phrase would be 'span of management' since the idea behind it is not concerned just with control but with all aspects of managing. The question of how many subordinates a manager can handle is one which has taxed all manner of people for a very long time. In fact, the problem is discussed in the *Old Testament* by Jethro, Moses' father-in-law, when Moses seemed to be spending all his time sorting out disputes.*

In modern times a number of attempts have been made to come up with a definite answer to the question. General Sir Ian Hamilton wrote in 1921 that between three and six is the ideal number, depending on the level in the organization.

Lyndall Urwick, the management consultant, considered five or six to be ideal towards the top; and at the lowest levels in the

---

* The whole episode is in *Exodus* xviii, 13–16.

organization it can be as many as twelve (if these twelve do not supervise the work of others).

Surveys have revealed that the number of managers reporting to the managing director varies from one to twenty-four, the average being eight or nine.

One piece of research – carried out by the Frenchman, V. A. Graicunas, in 1933 – examined the number of possible relationships that can exist within a group:

Mr X has two assistants, A and B. There is, therefore, a direct relationship between X and A and also between X and B. On occasions, however, Mr X will discuss things with A when B is also present, and sometimes he will discuss things with B when A is present. These two could be called 'group relationships'.

Moreover, there are times when A will want to discuss things with B, and others when B wants to consult A. These two could be called 'cross relationships'.

There are, therefore six possible relationships:

| Two direct relationships | + | Two group relationships | + | Two cross relationships |

The startling discovery is that if there were three subordinates, there could be a total of 18 relationships. If there were four subordinates, the total rises to forty-four. Beyond this, the numbers grow very fast:

Number of subordinates	Total number of relationships
1	1
2	6
3	18
4	44
5	100
6	222
7	490
8	1,080
9	2,376
10	5,210
20	10,486,154
24	201,327,166

Fortunately the chances of all the possible relationships occurring in any group on any one day are very remote. If this was attempted, chaos would result. As to the question of the effective number of subordinates which anyone can manage, bearing all this in mind – it must depend on the nature and complexity of the work and on the characters of the people involved.

Complex organizations

Eventually an organization which has successfully divided itself up on a simple basis will find itself with another problem that results from growth. This is known as the 'chain of command' and can be illustrated by the case of the firm which wanted a salesman to visit every hardware shop in Britain once every two weeks. The firm calculated that they needed a total of 2,160 salesmen to do the job properly. Bearing in mind the problem of the span of control, they decided to structure the operation as follows:

Six salesmen report to a territory manager;
Six territory managers report to an area manager;
Six area managers report to a regional manager;
Five regional managers report to a general sales manager;
Two general sales managers report to the sales director (who in turn reports to the managing director).

In total there are 432 managers and seven levels of responsibility. In other words, the chain of command has seven levels.

By being a little more flexible and deciding that one manager could comfortably manage twelve salesmen, a revised structure was drawn up with only six levels:

Twelve salesmen report to an area manager;
Nine area managers report to a regional manager;
Five regional managers report to a general sales manager;
Four general sales managers report to the sales director (who still reports to the managing director).

Now, having cut out one complete layer of management, the number of managers has been reduced to 204, and the conclusion from all this is that the wider the span of control, the shorter the chain of command. The problem with a very long chain of command is that instructions, questions, suggestions and requests take a long time to pass up and down the line, especially if there is no way of short-circuiting the process. This is wasteful of time, energy and money and, as a control system, would be inadequate.

The shorter the chain of command, the faster decisions are taken and the quicker any problems are solved. In addition, to be a long way from the top in terms of an organization chart results in a loss of morale – people begin to feel like numbers or 'cogs in a wheel' and rather insignificant.

The problem, then, for the increasingly complex organization, is how to divide itself up without losing the flexibility of the smaller firm and without creating a situation where the staff feel unimportant. Often the answer lies in the creation of self-contained divisions or separate businesses. We can see the difference between this and the simple departmental organization by looking at their respective organization charts:

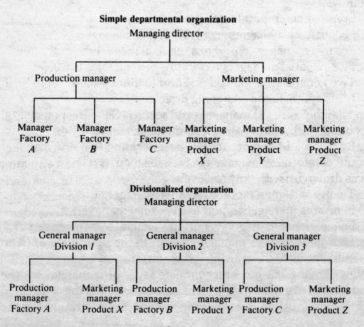

The importance of the product/factory relationship is that factory A makes product X; factory B would make product Y and factory C would make product Z.

In the divisionalized organization, the managing director is no longer concerned with coordinating the marketing and production functions of all the different products and factories. He has delegated that responsibility to each of the three general managers, therefore his role can now be much more strategic in emphasis and concerned with the overall performance and prospects of each division as a separate business.

However, there are some limitations to the divisional structure. It is not appropriate for single-activity organizations, however large. It could lead to under-utilization of some productive resources. The advantage of the departmental company is its ability to minimize waste and maximize capacity. Moreover, the divisionalized organization can spread talent too thinly across the company, whereas the departmental organization puts together all the expertise in a particular function.

Note: It is worth considering what might happen if, in an organization you know well, the work-load suddenly grew fourfold. Would the present structure cope? And if not, what structure would be most appropriate?

The matrix organization

An alternative type of organization structure which has come into prominence over the last thirty years is known as the 'matrix structure'. The idea is to avoid the weaknesses of both the departmental and the divisional structures. It has its roots in advertising agencies, construction companies and in civil and aeronautical engineering firms. Indeed you will come across it in all types of organizations which are engaged in projects – i.e. activities with a specific limited objective. However it can also be used in more standardized forms of activity.

The essence of a matrix structure is that the functional relationships within the business still stand. For example, there would still be a production manager with three factory managers reporting to him, as in the top chart opposite. However, each factory manager would have a direct relationship with his counterpart on the marketing side, rather than an indirect, informal contact. Using the charts on p. 30, the matrix organization structure appears like this:

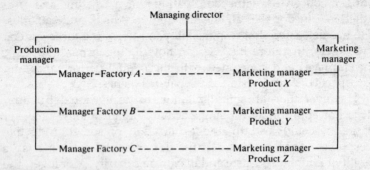

Each marketing manager would take on a coordinating responsibility for his particular product, ensuring that all aspects of its production, distribution, storage, promotion and sale were handled in the most efficient and profitable way. Similarly in companies engaged in project work, a project manager would be appointed to make sure that the project was a success. He would have a number of experts reporting to him as long as the project was in progress; as soon as it finished, all concerned would move on to a new job. In the same way, advertising agencies have account executives to manage each client organization's advertising needs.

The holding company

Ultimately an organization grows so large that the only effective way it can be managed is by making separate companies out of existing divisions. This can be done in such a fashion that the only relationship between each operating company and the top of the organization is the legal one of ownership – the divisions becoming 'wholly-owned subsidiaries'. The actual connections become mainly concerned with the movement of finance and the transfer of profits, and the head office only interferes if adequate profits are not being generated.

Many large companies operate self-contained divisions in this way, but do not go so far as to create separate legal entities; others only have legal subsidiaries when they buy up independent firms. Thus there can be a mixture of divisions and subsidiaries.

Centralization v decentralization

One of the most difficult questions to resolve in relation to the structure of large organizations is the extent to which authority should be kept at the top or passed down the line. In effect, this implies that if all the decisions are taken by the owner of a small business – or by the managing director of a large firm – then it may be described as a highly centralized operation. On the other hand, if the power to take decisions is passed down from the top, then it is a relatively decentralized organization. As we have seen, the owner of the small firm has to delegate; and the more he delegates, the more his firm is decentralized.

If the organization charts on p. 30 and 32 fairly represent actual authority, then it is easy to see that the departmental organization is still centralized, while the authority in the divisional company is passed down a level from the managing director to the divisional general managers. In the same way, in the matrix structure the authority must be decentralized to the project team leader if that kind of structure is to work effectively.

The line and staff problem

As we noted early in this chapter, it is normal in a small firm for the owner to hire in professional services as and when they are required. These services, such as legal and accounting, are essential, yet they are not directly connected with the production, distribution and sale of the firm's goods and services. They can be likened to the umpires, groundsmen and score-keepers at a cricket match: not actually in the game, but essential to its success. All organizations need the services of a variety of experts and as they grow, so they bring in more and more such people; these areas of expertise are usually referred to as 'staff functions'.

The accountancy function is one of the most important, because every transaction made has to be recorded and checked.

Also, the enormous sums of money flowing through organizations have to be carefully controlled. Finally, many decisions in organizations have a financial element and the accountancy function is best placed to help managers arrive at a sound decision. Accountants neither make nor sell the product, but without their expertise the organization could very easily run into financial difficulties.

Similarly, the need for experts in personnel, legal, purchasing, market research, computers, statistics and many other areas is vital for the continuing success of the organization as it develops.

In contrast, the makers and the sellers in an organization are known as 'line functions' because their authority is received straight 'down the line' in the chain of command.

Decentralized staff functions

The discussion on decentralization on p. 33 was in relation to the line functions of an organization. However, a separate problem exists with staff functions, because they can easily remain centralized while the operating parts of the organization are decentralized. For instance, many large organizations retain a central buying function even though the operating units do so independently. The advantages of such an arrangement are that it is possible to concentrate all the buying skills in one place and therefore maximum buying power is obtained. On the other hand, if buying is carried out locally decisions can be made faster, sudden problems can be quickly solved and the buyer will have a better knowledge of the needs of local operating managers. However, he will not have the power and leverage that a headquarters buyer can exert. So what does a company do?

Each organization has to choose whether or not to decentralize its staff functions – unless they are so specialized that it is obviously uneconomic to duplicate them across all parts of the organization. There is no right or wrong answer to this: it all depends on the needs of the individual concern.

What determines structure?

The way an organization is structured depends on:

- the type of business or activity
- the objectives of the organization
- size
- the strategies being pursued
- the policies of top management
- the values of the people in positions of power within the
  organization

Getting organized means making sure that the structure best matches all these factors. Unfortunately, the structure has to change as new opportunities arise, as old activities die away and as the organization itself develops and grows. Most of the time the changes to be made are small, but when major change occurs then it is necessary to undertake a major reorganization which will completely alter the structure. These times have been described as periods of revolution, in contrast with evolutionary periods when development and growth are not so fast.* The important thing to remember is that the organization which fails to adapt its structure to meet the requirements of new strategies and new circumstances is unlikely to be successful in the long run.

* 'Evolution and Revolution as Organizations Grow', Larry E. Greiner, *Harvard Business Review*, July–August 1972.

4 Useful Policies for Managers

In management the word 'policy' is used to describe agreed ways of running the organization. Policy has been described as a standing plan or set of rules which are used over and over again in relation to specific aspects of the firm's operations. Policy decisions are taken with regard to the objectives of the organization, its strategies and the personal values and beliefs of the people with senior executive power 'at the top'. In this chapter I will be looking at the key areas of choice which organizations might consider in their policy formulation activities and identifying some of the options available.

Marketing and sales policies

The key policy decisions in marketing and sales can be grouped together under a broad heading commonly called 'the marketing mix'; a convenient way of classifying the variables in this kind of policy-formulation is known as the 'four p's':

- *product*
- *place*
- *promotion*
- *price*

A successful marketing operation is one where the mix is working to its best advantage – namely, that the product is right, it is in the right place, at the right price and is being promoted in the right way.

'Product' policies

Quality This refers not just to the materials which are used for a product, but can also refer to the level of service being offered.

The decision you will need to make here is whether to offer products or services that correspond with the norm for the sector, or whether to offer something which is 'at the bottom end' of the market. Alternatively, your organization may choose to focus its efforts on the highest possible quality, becoming the 'Rolls-Royce' of the industry sector.

Product range From a manufacturing or operations point of view, a single product is ideal, since this makes planning easy and maximum productivity can be achieved. On the other hand, to offer a very wide range of products or services creates a very busy organization, attracting many more customers.

'Place' policies

In marketing, the term 'place' has a wide meaning. It refers not only to the precise place where a customer can go to buy the product or service, but includes such issues as the way in which the product is to be moved from the production area to the final selling point. Once you have taken the basic strategic decision, defining the market in broad terms, you will need to make a whole range of policy decisions – otherwise much of your time and effort will be wasted on debate and discussion.

To whom should we sell? The choice is often between the final consumer of the product or service, an agent, a wholesaler or a retail operation, although it is not always necessary to sell exclusively through any one of these.

How do we get the product to the customer? With physical goods, the choice of distribution method is between getting the products direct to the customer from the production unit and sending them to warehouses or stores. Your choice will be influenced by such factors as:

- distances involved
- the size of the loads
- extent to which the products are perishable
- relative costs

Market coverage It is not easy to decide on the extent to which a market should be covered. To be able to sell and distribute to every potential customer will be very expensive, but the competition and also the level of service you desire will influence your decision.

Which physical distribution system? This issue is a straight choice between rail, road, sea or air. Again there is no easy answer to the question. The policy you choose will depend on the product, the channel of distribution, distance, cost, the desired level of service and the extent to which your firm wants to keep control of its products while they are in transit.

'Promotion' policies

Promotion in the widest sense of the word is concerned with the whole issue of persuading the customer to choose one particular product or service over another. It is also concerned with creating a favourable climate of opinion about an organization, its products, services or specific events. Therefore, promotion goes on all the time in all walks of life, as people and institutions attempt to persuade others of their ideals, politics, beliefs and religions, as well as their goods and services.

Every manager is likely to get involved in promotion from time to time; your policy decisions will be concerned with how much promotion is carried out, and the precise way in which this is done.

Generally, promotion covers five elements:

- *advertising*
- *publicity*
- *selling*
- *sales promotion*
- *packaging*

Advertising The three key policy questions connected with advertising are:

- What is the advertising going to say (the message)?
- How much is going to be spent?
- Where are we going to advertise (the medium)?

Many advertising campaigns fail not because the design is poor, but because the message has not been clearly spelt out or the wrong medium is chosen. Advertising can be expensive, and when the message and the medium are not carefully selected the campaign is simply a waste of money.

Publicity This can be described as free advertising, i.e. where an organization gets its name mentioned in public without having to pay for a proper advertising campaign. It is now recognized as being an important supplement to aid advertising and many organizations devote a considerable amount of time and effort to cultivating potential sources of free publicity.

Publicity is important in the public sector as well as in business; for example, many councils employ public relations and publicity officers.

Many senior managers see one of their main functions as being of a public relations and publicity nature.

Selling Your main policy decisions in this area will relate to the precise use you make of sales-people. Are they merely order-takers, or should they be in effect 'technical consultants' – giving advice and even designing the product to suit the customer's needs?

Another important policy decision which you will have to make in relation to the sales-people is the question of a remuneration system. What proportion of their pay will be in the form of commission or bonus?

Sales promotion Sales promotion activities are designed to persuade customers to buy a product or service by offering something in return – whether it is a special discount or a chance to win a dream holiday. In order to select a sales promotion policy you should consider these questions: Should we use them at all? Might they harm our image? What kind of sales promotion is best for us?

Packaging Your two main policy decisions on packaging are: How often do we up-date the design of the packaging? What standard of packaging should be used – the minimum to do the job, or

expensive? There is no doubt that poor packaging turns customers away. How far the reverse is true is open to question.

'Pricing' policies

Whenever a product or service is made available for sale, one of
your most important decisions will be as to the price to be
charged. The basic question therefore is: At what level should our
prices be pitched? Too high a price may give the impression of
quality, yet no sales may result. On the other hand, a very low
price may bring in a great deal of business at very little profit.

Policies in purchasing and operations

In managing the buying side of an organization and in operations
management, there are a number of basic choices for you to make
about the way jobs are carried out, and it is vital that you settle
these at the outset because the costs of taking the wrong decision
– or failing to take the right decision in time – can wreck your
organization.

Purchasing policies

Choosing suppliers   There are two issues here. The first is: How
many suppliers should we have? The second is: How do we
choose which organizations will supply us?
   The advantages of a single supplier are:

■ often gives a better service;
■ gives a better price;
■ helps to build a good relationship and is therefore more likely
to assist in a crisis.

   In contrast, the advantages of having several suppliers are:

■ safety – if one supplier cannot deliver, another will be able to;
■ one supplier may be unable to supply all the different goods
you need;
■ you are able to shop around for the best terms being offered at
any one time.

Amongst the factors to consider when choosing suppliers are price, reliability, technical support, payment terms, the quality of the products, financial health and (by no means the least important) friendship.

Stockholding policy Some organizations operate a hand-to-mouth policy of saving money by only buying just before the goods are needed. This is known as the 'just in time' system. Its disadvantages are that the price may not be as good as if they had bought in bulk, and in inflationary times early buying can be profitable. Also there is a risk that supply may be interrupted, leaving the firm without essentials.

If you decide to 'buy to stock', there are further, consequent decisions to be made: How many days' or weeks' supply do we store – bearing in mind the cost and the possibility of (*a*) loss or (*b*) unwanted goods if demand falls? Where do we store the goods – centrally, or scattered in strategic locations? The answers again depend on the nature of your organization's activities and its strategies.

Operations policies

Product range A single product or service has the merit of being simple to manage and leads to high productivity. The problem is that it is risky having all your eggs in one basket and, as we discussed in relation to marketing 'product' policies, there are advantages in having a wide product range. The importance of the policy decision here is clear: without it there would be endless debate between operations managers and marketing managers.

Production quantities With any physical product there is a choice between (*a*) manufacture in anticipation of demand ('making to stock') and (*b*) making only to customers' orders. The first policy enables the firm to supply off-the-shelf and leads to high productivity through production planning. On the other hand, making to customers' orders avoids the costs of carrying stock, but can result in low productivity especially if demand is erratic. An intermediate policy adopted by some firms is to make components to stock and only assemble the final product when the order has been received.

Degree of mechanization An important early policy decision is the amount of equipment you use. Traditionally this question only applied to manufacturing industry, but nowadays all kinds of organizations need to set policy in this area, especially as the use of technology in offices and in other services is increasing rapidly. All managers should have a clear policy on the extent to which equipment will be used in their area of responsibility.

Financial policies

One of the characteristics of your job as a manager is that no matter what kind of organization you work in, you will have some degree of financial responsibility. Very often this amounts to no more than having an expenditure budget which relates to the department or function you manage. Most policies of a financial nature are settled by top management, yet it is important for all managers to understand these, since it is highly probable that their budgets are set as a result of policy decisions.

The important financial policies to be aware of are:

- *Control of working capital* Some firms insist on collecting money from customers as fast as possible, keeping stocks as low as possible and paying suppliers as slowly as possible. By doing so, bank overdrafts can be kept down, or money can be released for other purposes. Stocks, debtors and creditors are the elements of working capital and decisions like these affect most managers in one way or another.

- *Raising new money* To raise extra finance for growth, companies can ask the owners for more (by selling more shares), can plough back profits (instead of giving dividends to shareholders), or can borrow. The extent to which a firm borrows is the most important policy decision and will affect you as an operating manager, particularly if you wish to spend money on capital items such as equipment or machinery. If 'no borrowing' is the policy, then there may be a restriction on capital expenditure. This is referred to as 'capital rationing' and the manager who does his homework best and produces the best arguments is most likely to get his ration of money.

Policies in personnel management

There are four aspects in the management of what is termed the 'human resource', where you will need to make policy decisions. These are:

- *recruitment and selection*
- *pay and conditions*
- *training and development*
- *industrial relations*

Recruitment and selection

Recruitment of staff is chiefly concerned with three questions:

- What sort of people do we need?
- How are we going to get them?
- Where do we get them from?

What sort of people do we need?

This question is not so simple as it appears at first glance. Obviously an organization which does no planning is asking the question daily, as work fails to get done on time – if at all. However most organizations try to establish well in advance what their staffing requirements will be, through their personnel planning activities. If you are wise, you will do these things even if there is no formal corporate personnel planning system.

There are four policy decisions which make personnel planning easier:

1 *What sort of age profile do we want?* An example of this is the firm which never recruits anyone over the age of thirty, or the company which never employs people under that age.

2 *What qualifications are needed?* Some organizations may be prepared to take on anyone who has the ability and experience to do the job; others will insist on certain minimum professional qualifications.

3 *How much experience is needed?* Some firms prefer to train their staff from scratch, others buy in experienced people.

4 *Do we want people with potential?* If you hire staff who appear to be capable of taking on greater responsibilities, you are making an assumption about the future of your organization: that it is going to thrive. The risk with employing such people is that they may be in too much of a hurry and leave before the opportunity for promotion crops up.

How are we going to get them?

The policy choice built into this question is: Do we recruit the people we need when we need them, or do we try to develop our own staff in anticipation of need?

The first course of action has the advantage that you will probably get a better-qualified person than if the only people available are home-grown. Moreover, there is some argument for bringing in new people from outside as new blood is generally good for the body. The disadvantages are that it is often more expensive to obtain new staff than to promote existing personnel; also, there is a risk that the new staff member may not in the end be suitable for the job. A sensible policy regarding the recruitment of new staff is clearly needed, and this should minimize the chances of getting a dud – but even so, the risk is there.

In contrast, the advantages of the planned development policy are first, that it is cheaper; second, it increases your chances of getting the right type of staff for the job; and third, the person you appoint can be effective in the new post more quickly because there is little or no settling-in time. Finally, the prospects of promotion from within, if strong, may well provide a motive for better work.

The disadvantages of growing your own talent are:

■ the talent may leave after being trained;
■ it may produce an inward-looking top management team, which is short of ideas.

Where do we get them from?

The main policy decision on this question is: Should recruitment be open to all, or limited in some special way – for example, by only advertising in local newspapers.

Selection There can be innumerable rules regarding staff selection. I have already mentioned the main ones, but particular organizations will also have to develop policies about all kinds of selection matters such as racial or sex discrimination; health; working for a competitor, and even religion.

Termination It is essential for all organizations to have clear policies about dismissal and redundancy. Every employee must be informed as to the conditions under which they could be dismissed, and you must establish a policy for dealing with staff who are surplus to requirements – either because of a trade recession or because the nature of the work has changed. It is also worth deciding in advance if the policy on redundancy is 'first in, first out' or 'last in, first out'.

Pay and conditions

The major policy matters relating to this aspect of personnel management are fivefold:

- *general levels of pay*
- *merit awards*
- *profit-sharing*
- *fringe benefits*
- *working conditions*

General levels of pay While many private-sector organizations try to have general pay levels which are roughly similar to the 'going rate' for particular jobs, many other firms have a policy of deliberately paying higher (or lower) rates. The high-pay-rate policy will be found in an organization which believes it is only by paying high wages and salaries that it will get the best people. In contrast, a low-rate-of-pay policy is one where a firm has decided to take a fairly tough attitude towards pay increases, and works hard to keep awards in line with the general minimum.

Merit awards   It has long been recognized that some individuals work harder and have a higher quality of results than others. It is a matter of policy whether and how the work of individuals (such as salesmen) can be measured precisely. Here it is normal to give the salesman a small percentage of the value of every order over a certain minimum quantity. In the same way, if output exceeds a certain basic level in factories, those achieving the excess share a bonus.

The problem is more difficult in offices and in other situations where it is hard to identify diligence and superior work. For this reason many public service organizations have no merit award system, arguing that it is the diligent and 'better' employee who gets promoted.

Profit-sharing schemes   A popular form of bonus is to give all employees a share in the profits of the firm. This may be a fixed percentage of the profits, so that in a bad year no bonus would be given, but in a boom time the bonus could be high.

While everyone likes a free gift of money, some people feel that such a policy cannot be fair. Whether the sum is distributed on the basis of basic pay (e.g. five per cent of pay) or if it is a flat sum (e.g. £500 a head), someone is bound to complain. Someone else would complain if it was given purely on merit, of course.

Fringe benefits   It is a matter of policy whether an organization gives its employees any benefits in addition to basic pay. How many benefits and how far to go are important decisions which will be based on the following considerations:

■ Is it normal for the industry?
■ Is it the only way of attracting staff?
■ Is the profit likely to be higher if we give out many benefits?
■ Who in the firm will enjoy the benefits and who will be left out? What do we tell those who are left out?

Working conditions   While minimum health and safety standards are set out by law for people at work, standards of the actual working environment can vary enormously from one organization to another – not only in connection with health and safety factors, but also in respect of such matters as the location of the organization and the standard of decor, furniture and fittings. Here there are merits and demerits on both sides of the argument as to whether such considerations are to be fostered or ignored. Often the decision hangs on whether top management believes these elements to be important in recruiting, keeping and motivating staff.

Training and development

The training of staff depends to some extent on other policies in the personnel management area. If an organization intends to hire people for the job that needs to be done immediately, then any training is optional. On the other hand, firms which recruit in anticipation of need, or which have a policy of growing their own talent, will by definition have to get involved in training to a much greater extent.

There are several different types of training:

- for the immediate job to be done.
- in understanding the immediate environment of the employee.
- to prepare for promotion.
- for improvement in all-round efficiency and understanding.

In all these situations your organization will have to decide on the extent to which it proposes to encourage staff at all levels to develop. This depends mainly on the future needs of the organization, and also on how rapidly the environment is changing. A company at the forefront of technology (in information processing, for example) may find its staff being called upon to possess new skills and knowledge quite suddenly; this could be fatal if the firm had not been developing its key staff in anticipation.

Training and development of managers This needs particular emphasis. There are many good reasons for putting considerable effort into it, but you must establish a policy as to how much management development your firm will undertake.

Performance appraisal Performance appraisal systems are being used increasingly to help improve the current performance of staff to assess training and development needs and also to assess future potential for promotion. Not all organizations carry out appraisal of any kind, but those employing such techniques are convinced of their value. Even if your company has no policy on the matter, if you are a manager who is in charge of other managerial or supervisory grades, you should find out how to carry out appraisal interviews and formulate your own policy on the subject.

Industrial relations

Policy on industrial relations depends on many factors such as the tradition of the industry and the size of the organization. In essence, industrial relations policy matters are concerned with the relationships between the organization and trade unions or other staff representatives.

The choices that exist for you as manager can best be seen by considering a number of specific questions which you will have to answer if you wish to have sound rules for negotiation:

■ To what extent do we want our staff to have their pay and conditions negotiated by trade unions?
■ What should our attitude towards the unions be?
■ How far should we involve the unions?
■ In the event of a dispute, how far should we try to avoid damaging industrial action?

Whatever your answers to these questions, you must bear in mind the overall reason for policy in industrial relations – namely that your organization is seeking an efficient and effective method of ensuring that staff at all levels are treated fairly as regards pay and conditions.

Last words on policy

Although it is the responsibility of senior managemnt to develop policies on a wide range of their organization's activities, you should try to understand the thinking behind policy decisions whatever your position. You should also remember that policies should not be cast in concrete and kept for ever. As your organization and its environment change, so policies will also need to be altered and it is you, the manager, who are best placed to advise the policy-makers of the changes which become necessary. Therefore, all managers have a hand in policy formulation and should be prepared both to advocate a policy where one is needed and to amend one which is out of date.

5 Leadership and Motivation

Managers often have to take on the leadership role and this automatically involves motivating people. Many different views exist on the subject, and in this chapter we will consider some of the leading theories of motivation and outline their main features.

There was once a farmer who bought a donkey from a neighbour. The following morning he went to its stable, saddled it up as best he could – since it was sitting down on the straw – and then tried to make it stand up and walk into the farmyard. Sad to relate, no matter what he did he could not get the donkey to move. He talked to it; he whispered in its ear; he cursed it; he offered it carrots and candy (which it ate). He beat it with a stick, but all in vain; it would not budge.

Finally he phoned the neighbour, who said he would come over and fix things straight away. A little while later the neighbour arrived in the farm carrying a large sledgehammer. Going into the stable where the donkey was sitting peacefully, he walloped it over the head with the hammer. Immediately the beast rose and walked into the yard, where it backed into the cart and stood waiting to be harnessed to it.

'That's amazing,' said the farmer. 'Why did he respond when you hit him on the head?'

'That's easy,' replied the neighbour. 'All he needed was the right motivation.'

There is not much doubt that most people would not be motivated in the same way as the donkey, yet it is odd that sometimes even the most tempting offers fail to have the desired effect on humans. The need for motivating people is not seriously under question; it is acknowledged to be important. The problem is how to achieve it, recognizing at the same time that it can be destroyed very easily.

One way of looking at the question is to ask yourself what situation at work would cause you to lose completely any motivation you might have for your job. What would cause you to give up trying, to do the minimum required of you, and eventually to leave?

There are, of course, a number of answers to this. To have your pay cut in half would do the trick very nicely! So might making you work outdoors in all kinds of weather (if you now work inside). You might well lose motivation if you were asked to do something illegal or against your principles; or if your boss started insulting you and maligning your character; or again if you were continually being held responsible for things going wrong which had nothing to do with you. Some people are demotivated if there is no challenge in what they are doing, if the work is boring, or if they cannot see the purpose behind their job. All these and many more are possible ways of becoming demotivated, of losing the will and inclination to do more than the absolute minimum.

However, what is the situation if we turn the question on its head and ask about motivation and not *de*motivation? Think back to a time when you were performing really well and ask yourself what were the factors which brought about your high level of performance? It may have been something to do with the job itself – interesting, exciting or challenging, for example. It may have been because of pay and conditions – a very good wage or a very comfortable place to work. It may have been that your colleagues were a 'great crowd' – you enjoyed their company and they enjoyed yours.

Another possibility is that the organization itself seemed to be the kind of set-up in which it was a pleasure to work; the atmosphere inside and the image outside all contributed to a morale-boosting environment.

Finally, it could have been the individual or people for whom you were working or – to give it a fancier title – the leadership style of the people in charge. Words which spring to mind here might include trust, encouragement, recognition, consultation and freedom.

It would seem, therefore, that there are a number of things

which could turn people off their jobs, and an equal number of things which could turn them on. Oddly, the factors which turn people off are not always the opposite of those which turn them on. For instance, although a cut in pay may easily demotivate someone, a big pay rise will not necessarily cause them to work any harder or better.

So, motivation is a very complex question and there is no magic formula which can be universally applied. Over the years many people have pondered the problem and suggested solutions – some of which seem to work better than others. In the following pages I will consider some of the key personalities in the debate and discuss their ideas. To begin with, we shall have to go back nearly 200 years to the early days of the Industrial Revolution.

Robert Owen

Although there is nowadays a view that Robert Owen was paternalistic, there is no doubt that this Welshman was way ahead of his time. During the early years of the nineteenth century, his textile mill at New Lanark in Scotland was the scene of some novel ways of treating people. His view was that people at work are not all that different from machines; if a machine is looked after, cared for and maintained, then it is likely to be more efficient, reliable and longer-lasting than equipment which is neglected. Similarly, people at work are likely to be more efficient and reliable if they are well looked after than if they are treated badly. Robert Owen practised what he preached and introduced such things as employee housing and a company shop. His ideas on this and other matters were too revolutionary for the times, and many of his innovations were opposed.

Jeremy Bentham

Possibly the essence of the traditional view of people at work can be best appreciated by a brief look at this English philosopher whose ideas were also developed in the early years of the Industrial Revolution, around 1800. Bentham's view was that all people are self-interested and are motivated by the desire to avoid pain and find pleasure. Thus, an individual will work only if the reward is big enough, or the possible punishment sufficiently unpleasant. This view – the 'carrot and stick' approach – was built into the philosophies of the age and is still to be found today, especially in the older and more traditional sectors of industry.

Elton Mayo

The work of Elton Mayo represents a significant landmark in the development of ideas about the behaviour and attitudes of people at work. Mayo was born in 1880 – forty-eight years after Bentham died – and although trained as a psychologist in Australia, he eventually moved to the United States where in 1926 he became a professor of industrial research at the Harvard Graduate School of Business. Two years before this, he had begun the series of experiments which have become so famous and which are now referred to as the Hawthorne Experiments.

The Hawthorne Works of the American Western Electric Company was in Chicago, where over 30,000 people were employed in making telephone equipment. Mayo and his team were called in because, in spite of many 'progressive' employee schemes in the firm (such as a pension scheme and other facilities), there was poor productivity and a good deal of dissatisfaction. The idea behind the first experiment was that if conditions of work improve, so will productivity. Therefore, it was decided to start by improving the lighting for a group of female employees.

To be sure that the results were scientific, a 'control' group was set up – another team of employees whose lighting would not be changed. Nobody was surprised when the output of the experimental team increased, but everyone was very surprised to discover that the output of the second 'control' group had also risen. The lighting continued to be improved and output continued to rise. Then came the second big surprise, when the lighting was gradually reduced but output still rose. Eventually it got so dark that hardly anything could be seen at all – at that point, at last, output dropped.

Further experiments over several years all pointed in the same direction. Five-minute rest pauses were introduced and output rose. Then these were extended to ten minutes and output rose significantly. However, when six five-minute pauses a day were introduced, output fell and the girls complained that their work rhythm was being interrupted too often. When the two-rest-pauses system was reintroduced with a free hot meal during one of them, output went up again. Later the girls were sent home at 4.30 instead of 5.00 p.m. and output rose, but when they were sent home at 4.00 p.m. output stayed the same. Finally, all the improvements were withdrawn and the group went back to the situation as it had been at the beginning. This produced the most startling result of all – output rose yet again, ending over thirty per cent higher than it had been at the start of the experiments.

The unexpected phenomenon arising from these experiments is known as the Hawthorne Effect – this effect being that there is something else which determines an individual's productivity besides working conditions and personal well-being. The girls at the Hawthorne Works knew that they were being involved in some experiments which were of interest to the management. Throughout the experiments an observer sat with the girls and kept them informed of what was going on and how the experiments were doing, also listening to their comments and complaints. The view now is that the girls responded to the interest being shown in them and their work. Although Mayo's researches have been criticized from many angles, there is not much argument about his central conclusions, namely:

- people are motivated by more than pay and conditions;
- the need for recognition and a sense of belonging are very important;
- attitudes towards work are strongly influenced by the group (since work is frequently a group activity).

A. H. Maslow

Maslow developed his Theory of Human Motivation in the early 1940s. Until then – apart from the ideas we have looked at so far – most of the work on motivating people had been confined to economists and psychologists like Freud, Adler and Jung. Maslow's idea was that there are many human needs, and that motivation comes from an individual's desire to satisfy these. He classified the needs into a 'hierarchy' (i.e. grades) as follows:

1 *Physiological needs* These are basic and include the need to satisfy hunger and thirst. In some societies these primary needs are not totally satisfied, but in most industrial economies the vast majority of people do not have to concern themselves too much with them. Once these needs have been satisfied, they no longer operate as motivators and people focus on others.

2 *Safety needs* In Maslow's terms, safety not only consists of the kind of safety which comes from a fear of being attacked, but also shelter, clothing and protection from all potentially dangerous or uncomfortable things such as the weather, machinery, vehicles, fire and flood.

As well as the physical safety factors, there are also psychological safety factors which are considered to be very important motivators. Psychological safety includes pensions, health insurance, unemployment benefits and the need to avoid being out of work.

3 *Affection (or social) needs* The need for affection and love can be described as the social need to belong to a group – not only the family, but also the group in which the individual works (or plays). It has been noticed that loyalty to a small work group and the need to belong to the group can weigh heavily in discussions about changing an organizational set-up.

4 *Esteem needs* The need for esteem includes self-respect and the feeling that something useful has been accomplished. In addition, esteem includes the need to receive recognition for what has been done and to have someone express their appreciation.

5 *Self-actualization needs* Maslow used the expression 'what a man can be, he must be', which really means that this need is concerned with self-fulfilment – being able to do what you really

want to do. Examples of this can be found in music, in art and in sport, where people spend all their time and energy involved in the things they most love doing.

Although Maslow's theory assumes that individuals will seek to satisfy the lower-level needs before moving on up the hierarchy, it is worth noting that there are many examples of individuals who are more concerned about higher needs and pay little attention to the more basic ones. In most people, there is a mixture of needs at any time; some will be stronger than others.

Frederick Herzberg

The work of Dr Herzberg is more recent than that of Maslow, his findings only being made widely known towards the end of the 1950s. Herzberg was interested in the question of 'job satisfaction'. Specifically, several hundred accountants and engineers were interviewed and asked about the way in which incidents at work affected the way they felt about their jobs. From the answers, Herzberg developed his theory that there are two factors at work in determining job satisfaction. He called them:

- *hygiene factors*
- *motivators*

According to Herzberg, hygiene factors include pay, working conditions, pension funds and fringe benefits. He made the point that these factors have to be present and adequate, otherwise there can be job dissatisfaction. On the other hand, an abundance of hygiene factors does not necessarily lead to a highly motivated staff.

'Motivators', on the other hand, are the positive factors which have to be present if there is to be job satisfaction. These are associated with such things as responsibility, a sense of achievement, challenge and self-improvement. In other words, all these factors motivate people to work effectively, and without them – no matter how good the hygiene factors – there will be no improvements in productivity and efficiency.

Another interesting conclusion drawn from the studies was

that so long as the motivators are present in abundance, people will tolerate all kinds of deficiencies in the hygiene factors.

Douglas McGregor

McGregor's book, *The Human Side of Enterprise*, first appeared in 1960 (published by McGraw-Hill). In it he describes two extreme views about the way people inside organizations are managed. There is the traditional view, which he calls Theory X, and a more modern view, Theory Y.

Theory X

Every management decision is taken with the assumption of certain specific views about human nature and behaviour. These are:

- that the average human being has an inherent dislike of work and will avoid it if possible;
- that most people have to coerced, controlled, directed and threatened with punishment in order to get them to make an effort in the direction of the organization's goals;
- that the average human being dislikes responsibility and has little ambition, prefers being directed and wants security first and foremost.

McGregor points out that most organizations provide for the physiological and safety needs of their employees. This being the case, he asserts that staff will be seeking to satisfy higher-level needs and if they do not succeed in this aim, then it is not surprising that they behave in the ways suggested above – with indolence, passivity, resistance to change and unwillingness to take responsibility.

Theory Y

There are a number of basic assumptions about human behaviour which McGregor uses to support this theory:

- that physical and mental effort at work is as natural as rest or play out of work;
- that threats of punishment and controls are not the only ways to achieve the goals of the organization. People do exercise self-control and self-direction if they are committed to those goals;
- that the average human being is willing to seek out and take responsibility under certain circumstances (note here McGregor's qualifying words 'average' and 'certain circumstances');
- that many (not a few) people are capable of exercizing a lot of imagination, ingenuity and creativity in solving the problems of the organization;
- that as things are organized at present, the average human's brain-power is being only partially used.

An organization run on Theory X lines tends to be authoritarian in nature, the word 'authoritarian' suggesting such ideas as the 'power to enforce obedience' and 'the right to command'. In contrast, a Theory Y organization can be described as 'participative', where the aims of the organization and of the individuals in it are integrated, i.e. individuals can best achieve their own goals by directing their efforts towards the success of the organization.

Theory X and Theory Y have come in for considerable criticism, mainly on two counts. First of all, both theories involve making wide generalizations about work and human behaviour. Theory X has been described as 'organizations without people' and Theory Y as 'people without organizations'. The two theories represent extremes, and such generalizations do not fairly represent what is actually going on; it has been established that few people correspond precisely with the descriptions set out in either theory. Secondly, it is clear that to have Theory X-type organization does not automatically lead to failure; conversely, a Theory Y set-up is no guarantee of success.

Rensis Likert

While Theories X and Y represent extreme views, Likert has developed a refined classification which breaks down organizations into four management systems:

- system 1: primitive authoritarian
- system 2: benevolent authoritarian
- system 3: consultative
- system 4: participative

Likert believes that most firms are somewhere between system 2 and system 3, and that research confirms the view that as organizations move nearer to system 4 so their results improve.

Victor Vroom

The work of Victor Vroom and others in the 1960s has led to the development of an even more sophisticated theory of motivation, now known as the Expectancy Theory. This suggests that two separate things need to be working so as to motivate an individual. First, there is the usual view that people want things; they want not only the basic things in life, but many other things like promotion, status, power and so on. Some of these 'wants' are strong desires, but others will be merely a 'liking' for something. The relative strength of someone's preference for one thing as against another is called the 'valance'. So that if we say, 'promotion has a high valence for Joe', what we mean is that Joe wants promotion very much indeed.

The second element in the motivation equation is called the 'expectancy', which is a person's own estimation of his chances of achieving what he wants. Thus 'I'll never get promotion' is a statement reflecting a very low expectancy.

The important thing about Expectancy Theory is that it sees motivation as similar to an electric current. If the strength of the current is too low, there is not enough power in it to make a motor turn. In the same way, motivation has to reach a certain strength in order to lead to action. Hence:

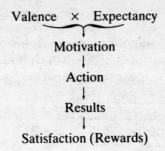

The importance of the X sign between valence and expectancy is this: if either of the two items is absent (or negative), then no motivation can possibly result.

Clayton Alderfer

Alderfer's work is recent, but is considered significant. It is called the ERG Theory, the letters standing for three different kinds of need: Existence; Relatedness; Growth. This is similar to Maslow's list, but in three groups instead of five. Moreover, instead of seeing the needs as a hierarchy, Alderfer considers them to be a continuum along which people move all the time:

Existence	*Relatedness*	*Growth*
Material desires (physiological needs; security; money)	People relationships (social and esteem needs)	Self-actualization (creative desires)

Motivation and the work group

One of the important elements in many of the theories about motivation is the work group. Indeed, one of the conclusions of the Hawthorne experiments was that belonging to the group is a strong motivating force in its own right. A work group may be a small two- or three-person team, or it may be a large department in a factory or office. In the world of music it ranges from a group of four musicians (like the Amadeus Quartet or the Beatles) to the 1,000 singers and players normally required for a performance of Mahler's Eighth Symphony. At either extreme, the members of the group are all pursuing a common goal.

In music-making, if one or two members fail to perform as well as the rest, the performance suffers as a whole. The same effect can be seen in team sports, and indeed is true of any work group although it may not be quite so obvious as in music or sport. The effect is known as failing to live up to the group norms and, as found in the Hawthorne Experiments, there can be a very strong pressure on individuals to adjust to and accept these norms.

Group atmosphere

Research has demonstrated that the atmosphere of a group often has a considerable influence on the performance of individuals within it, and therefore on the performance of the group as a whole. There are many aspects to the concept of a group atmosphere, but they include the notions of:

- friendliness
- enthusiasm
- supportiveness
- warmth
- satisfaction
- interest
- productivity
- cooperation
- success

Group work

An interesting example of group work is that of Volvo Motors in Sweden. The management at Volvo saw that, in the conveyor-belt method of making cars, each worker sees only a tiny fraction of the whole process. Because he is doing a repetitive job he eventually gets bored; he cannot see the end product of his labours. To overcome this group working was introduced, whereby a small team of workers could together be responsible for the output of a particular department or workshop – all members of the department being encouraged to learn each other's jobs. This is known as 'multi-skilling' and can lead to an increase in motivation because jobs have a broader aspect and therefore are less boring. Also productivity rises because the absence of a single member of the team does not now hold up the whole process.*

Motivation and the job itself

If responsibility, self-fulfilment and achievement are motivators, then doing a boring, repetitive job is unlikely to be a highly motivating experience. 'Job design', as it is called, works on the assumption that these motivating factors should be built into the job, whether or not it is done as part of a group working scheme. A concern for the quality of working life (QWL) is increasingly being seen as an important contribution to greater efficiency, and the two expressions which have come into prominence in this area are:

■ *job enrichment* and
■ *job satisfaction*

Job enrichment

This is also sometimes called job enlargement, and is the process of making jobs more interesting by increasing the amount of responsibility each individual has and giving them greater opportunities for self-development. Many of the ideas about job enrichment come out of the motor-car industry, where studies revealed a high degree of boredom, a low level of job satisfaction and considerable dislike of the work. This was because the speed of the assembly line determined the pace of work; the skills needed were minimal and therefore the individuals felt isolated.

Especially when built into group-working schemes, job enrichment has been seen to have beneficial effects, but you should

* For a review of this, see the *Financial Times*, 19 April 1985: 'The Volvo Experiment ten years on'.

remember that the success of such a programme will depend on the background and attitudes of the individuals involved.

Job satisfaction

This has already been considered in connection with the work of Herzberg (p. 56). There are many more studies in this area, and those which have tried to establish a relationship between job satisfaction and productivity are especially interesting. It seems that job satisfaction comes from doing a job well. However, it also appears to be the case that unless an individual's work is designed to be satisfying, then high productivity is unlikely to result. Good job performance leads to job satisfaction and this leads to even better performance, leading in turn to even more job satisfaction. Conversely, poor job performance leads to less job satisfaction and this, in turn, results in worse job performance and even lower job satisfaction, etc.

Leadership style

Successfully leading an organization or part of an organization is one of the hallmarks of the effective manager. By definition, real leadership implies the willingness of others to follow or – as we saw in Chapter 1 (p. 4) – to be directed. If leadership is poor, or absent, the individuals in the group or organization will display all the characteristics associated with low motivation; they are not willing followers and will only perform to the minimum standards. In contrast, if the quality of leadership is high, the motivation and performance of members of the organization or group will also be high.

These effects can be seen, for example, in the management of football teams, where the performance of the team is tied up very closely with the team manager's own leadership skills. The team lacking a manager or with a weak manager performs less well than teams with stronger managers. It is worth noting, however, that sometimes a successful manager who transfers to another club finds that his successful leadership formula no longer works.

This kind of experience is found in every organization; sometimes a manager is a success and sometimes he is not, and this seems to have a lot to do with leadership style in combination with the organization's own values, beliefs, culture and requirements.

Leadership style means the way in which the leader of the group relates to his or her subordinates; there are a number of ways to classify these styles. Some divide them into two broad categories: the leader who is oriented towards people, as distinct from the leader who is orientated towards the job in hand and getting it done.

People-centred leadership

An extreme view of a people-centred leader would be the manager who strives above all to make the individuals for whom he is responsible feel that their needs are being looked after. The aim of such managers is to run a 'happy ship', on the principle that if all the members of the crew are happy then it will be easy to sail the ship in the right direction.

Work-centred leadership

A totally work-centred leadership style would probably correspond to Theory X (p. 57) and might well be described as 'scientific management' – a concept which was examined in Chapter 1 in connection with the work of F. W. Taylor (p. 5).

These two styles represent extreme views and clearly there are many others. An alternative classification was suggested by two writers, Tammenbaum and Schmidt, in 1958* and it is a classification which has gained considerable support. It has been described as a 'leadership continuum' and embodies a range of styles including:

- autocratic – where the leader dictates what he wants;
- persuasive – where the leader sells his ideas, using the morale and enthusiasm of the team members;

* 'How to Choose a Leadership Pattern', *Harvard Business Review*, March–April 1958.

- consultative – where the leader discusses with the team members, but then takes the decision himself;
- democratic – where the leader involves team members in discussion and in decision.

The full continuum can be illustrated like this:

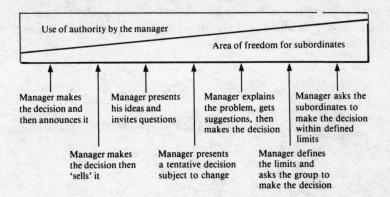

The appropriate style of leadership to use for maximum motivation will depend on a number of factors:

- the size of the organization;
- whether or not the work-force is highly skilled;
- whether there is a high degree of interaction between members of the group;
- the personalities of the members of the group;
- the knowledge and ability of the leader;
- how quickly decisions need to be made;
- what the team members feel most comfortable with;
- the current state of the organization (how well is it doing?);
- the normal style of the organization.

A good example of differing leadership styles is given by Sir Winston Churchill in his book *The Second World War*. He describes how General Montgomery would not eat with his subordinates, but would have a sandwich by his car. Napoleon would also have kept apart (but eaten better!), whereas both Marlborough and

Cromwell would have fed with their officers. The techniques may have differed but the results, says Churchill, were the same.

Action-centred leadership

Another very useful way of looking at leadership, developed by John Adair,* is called action-centred leadership and is illustrated by this diagram:

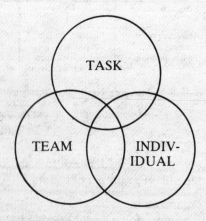

The leader's role is threefold:

- define and achieve the task
- build and maintain the team
- develop the individuals

'Task' is concerned with such things as setting objectives and determining strategy and tactics. 'Team' refers to the group and ensuring that it operates as a cohesive unit, pulling together and with the members supporting each other. The 'Individuals' aspect relates to motivation, education and training in the members of the group, so that each is confident, competent and capable. If any one of the three aspects is underdeveloped or

* See *Effective Leadership* by John Adair, Pan Books, 1984.

neglected, then it is very difficult – if not impossible – to achieve desired results.

Face-to-face leading

One important aspect of every manager's job as leader is the way in which individuals are addressed, both in speech and in writing. Consider these two examples:

- 'Your trouble, Smith, is that you don't seem to want promotion and you don't push hard enough. Don't let people push you around so much.'
- '*To all salesmen:* You are reminded that you must inform my office of your movements before setting out on your journeys. Failure to do so could lead to loss of commission.'

Neither of these two statements seems very encouraging or helpful, and may well have a demotivating effect on the recipients. Yet you will probably see and hear this kind of communication every day. Good managers who motivate their staff pick their words carefully and avoid being as negative as in the above examples – even though the speaker in the first does actually seem to be trying to help. Obviously there are times when individuals or groups have to be told unpleasant things. At such times most people would appreciate straight talking and prefer to be treated like adults. There are techniques – such as Transactional Analysis – which are concerned with looking at different ways of saying the same thing; they show how the right choice of words can avoid annoying, upsetting or depressing the listener: all part of motivation.

6 Decision-making and Problem-solving

Managers have to make decisions; it is their responsibility. Moreover, the problems which seem to beset all managers often cannot be ignored or passed on; it is their responsibility to solve them. This chapter is concerned with describing the process of problem-solving and explaining how good decision-making works.

A simple way of thinking about decision-making is to relate it to the fairly common experience of deciding what to eat in a restaurant. Usually you are presented with a menu which identifies the choices available to you and the price you will have to pay. Your choice will be determined with reference to some pre-set rules or limiting factors like how hungry you are; who is paying for the meal; the prices of the dishes; what you like and dislike. Often there are two or three items which you are fond of and want to order; the problem is to choose one, especially when you are holding up the others around the table. In the end, your decision might be based on the fact that you had not eaten one particular item for some time, or that someone had recommended the dish to you.

For present discussion, the actual decision itself is not as important as the way in which you reached it. In the process of making the decision, a number of distinct steps can be identified:

Step 1 Identify a problem which it is your responsibility to solve.
Step 2 Find out the facts.
Step 3 Look for some solutions.
Step 4 Narrow the choice of alternatives.
Step 5 Take the decision.
Step 6 Implement the decision.

The process of arriving at a decision is usually referred to as 'problem solving' and there are many ways in which the steps can be classified. However, all will include the following basic elements, which correspond to the six steps listed above:

- Recognize that there is a problem.
- Diagnose the cause or causes.
- Develop some possible solutions.
- Evaluate the possibilities.
- Choose (i.e. take the decision).
- Implement.

Each of these elements needs more detailed consideration.

1 Recognize a problem

The dictionary defines 'problem' as a 'doubtful or difficult question' and it would be very nice if all problems were presented to us on paper in the form of a question. For instance, consider this question:

> The word icedions is an anagram of what?

This is a problem; it is written down in the form of a question which has to be considered and given some thought. Unfortunately it is very rare for a manager to receive his problems like that; usually he receives them like this:

> In this carpeth you need to use your arbin.

At first glance the sentence is meaningless because there are two words in it you do not recognize. Immediately a question forms in your mind: What do the words mean? At that moment, you recognize that you have a problem.

In exactly the same way, a manager receives information which does not make sense or does not ring true in some way. It may be obvious that there is a problem. 'John, John. The warehouse is on fire!' is instantly recognizable as a problem. Other problems, however, tend to creep up on to the manager without his realizing that he has a problem. For example, he may receive the following information from a salesman: 'The XYZ Company has decided to start advertising on TV.' If the manager has his wits about him he may well decide to check out that story, because if correct it could spell out a big competitive challenge. It is not a problem now, but it might become one very soon.

The very first thing to do on receiving some information, therefore, is to find out if it is actually a problem. Everyone does this all the time with the information they receive, but usually it occurs subconsciously and it is not necessary actually to ask the question out loud. This is because most information we receive is not in conflict with what we expect. It is only where some information conflicts with our knowledge or experience that mental alarm bells ring, and this is what happened when you read the words 'carpeth' and 'arbin' above. There is, however, a grey area where the alarm bell is very muted and it is then that it is important to have asked this question: Is there a problem?

The second part of this step is to ask the question: Is it really my problem? Too often, managers find that they are handling problems that are really someone else's responsibility. This can happen in many ways, one of the commonest being where a subordinate refers a problem upwards to his boss, in spite of having full authority to take a decision (and probably knowing the answer too). 'Passing the buck' is a favourite pastime in large organizations, but a good manager will encourage his subordinates to solve their own problems and settle their own differences. A weak manager, however, finds that he is being invited to look at, comment on, get involved with and generally waste time on problems which others are perfectly capable of handling.

2 Diagnose the cause(s)

It is one thing to be able to recognize that there is a problem, but an entirely different matter to be able to identify its basic cause. For instance, the strange word used on p. 69, 'carpeth', is an easily identified problem. We can tell from experience that the cause is that the letters of a real word have been mixed up, and this particular type of problem is called an anagram.

Since most problems encountered by managers are not so easily labelled this diagnosis stage is very important, as getting it wrong can easily lead to the wrong decision. Snap diagnosis is to be avoided: be sure to find out the basic cause of the problem. Ascertain the facts.

Spring Clamps (1): a case for diagnosis:
John Brown arrived at the office a few minutes after 9 a.m. on Monday. On his desk was this note from the supervisor of the morning shift:

> John,   8.35
>
> *Nearly all this week's supply of spring*
> *clamps are no use – if we don't get some*
> *more we'll have to shut the line at 2 p.m.*
>
>   Ted

John immediately went down to the stores and examined the clamps, which had been delivered during the previous week in accordance with the terms of the contract his firm had with the suppliers. Sure enough, they were nearly all faulty.

He returned to his office in a bad temper. 'Get me Fred Smith at Spring Clamps right away. It's very urgent,' he said to his young secretary, who was a bit irritated by this tone of voice and went off to phone feeling none too happy herself.

Fred Smith was an old friend of John's and as the firm was only twenty miles away there was a good chance of getting some more clamps over by 2 p.m. At about 10 o'clock John's secretary came into his office and announced that she had been having difficulties in getting through to Spring Clamps Ltd. However, she had just managed to speak to Fred Smith's secretary, who said that Mr Smith was not in and she did not know where he was. 'Keep trying,' said John. 'I must speak to him soon. I've got the Safety Committee in my office at 10.15, so pull me out of it as soon as you get him.'

The meeting ended without interruption at 11.30 and John's secretary continued to try to contact Fred Smith whenever there was a free line – John's incoming calls being particularly heavy that morning.

At 12.30 John sent his secretary to lunch, tried Spring Clamps Ltd himself and discovered that both Fred and his secretary were at lunch. So he left a message with Fred's assistant, telling him the problem and asking that Fred phone him instantly on his return.

Then John ordered up some sandwiches from the canteen and sat glowering at the telephone, wondering how to keep the production line going after 2 p.m.

At this point two important factors can be identified:

(i) The problem (at 12.30) is that it looks as though the production line will stop at 2 p.m. because the supply of spring clamps will be exhausted. Turning this into a question: How can we get hold of more spring clamps to keep us going after 2 p.m.?

(ii) The basic cause of the shortage is either (a) not enough were delivered, or (b) those which were received were faulty.

Since the correct quantity was delivered but the quality was wrong, they cannot have been inspected when they arrived. In other words, the crisis should never have occurred; the fault should have been noticed last week and dealt with there and then. The basic cause, therefore, is inefficient inspection on delivery.

It is possible to identify a whole string of secondary problems: arriving after 9 a.m. when the shop-floor people start earlier is one which springs to mind. So is the question of being irritable with a secretary, or not giving her full instructions, or continuing with a meeting when there is an urgent problem. In addition, there is the difficulty of trying to get hold of one particular individual in an organization. Does John have to speak to Fred and Fred alone?

In thinking through the diagnosis, what emerges is that there are two main problems, not one. There is the immediate problem of sorting out the shortage so that production can carry on after 2 p.m., and there is the second problem of finding a way to ensure that the same situation never arises again.

The whole process of diagnosis is best appreciated by considering the example of a doctor. Often, by listening to the patient's explanation of the problem, the doctor can diagnose the complaint. Indeed, a good explanation of a problem is often a sufficient diagnosis in any situation.

How to get a good explanation of a problem:

■ Write it down.
■ Turn it into language you can understand.

- Turn it into numbers if possible, using graphs and diagrams.
- Get a good information system, i.e. a way of making sure that facts are fed to you regularly and systematically.
- Avoid classifying the problem too soon (e.g. as an industrial relations problem or a marketing problem; these are risky assessments to make early on, because they limit your thinking).
- Ask questions such as: What caused such-and-such to happen? Why did it happen? What possible causes could there be?

The aim of this part of the exercise is therefore to be able to state clearly:

- *the problem*
- *the cause of the problem*
- *a restatement of intention or aim*

At the end of the case of the spring clamps, John Brown was left staring at the telephone. He knew what the problem was and he soon knew the cause. Then came his restatement of intent: 'I must find a way of keeping the production line going and then I must find a way to prevent it happening again.' At this point, he moves on to the next stage of the exercise.

3 Develop some possible solutions

This stage in the exercise involves the use of the brain, i.e. we have to do a bit of thinking, which we may or may not enjoy depending on the nature of the problem. Some people love crossword puzzles and enjoy considering how to solve them; others cannot bear such things and do not even attempt to think about them. Unfortunately managers have no choice – they have to solve the problems they are set, whether they like them or not. So the first thing to be sure about is that, to be an effective manager you will have to do some difficult thinking from time to time.

Developing solutions to problems means having some ideas, and there are all kinds of examples of how people have had their ideas. It is generally agreed that once the information has been gathered and a clear aim has been established, there comes a stage which has been called 'incubation' where the individual plays around with the information, trying to work out how it might solve the problem. For instance, with an anagram we may write down the letters in a different order two or three times, to see if the answer comes up. Another process that can be useful here is to let the subconscious mind take over. This can follow a period of active thinking about a problem when no obvious solution turns up. People have been known to go for a long walk, go to bed or do something totally different, and then to find on returning to the problem that 'the answer is there staring me straight in the face'. Such moments have been called 'the flash of insight' or 'moment of inspiration'; when they come up, they can save a lot of time and effort.

Consider two ways of solving the anagram 'ucer'. Either we can just look at it and hope to see the answer in a flash; or we can write down all twenty-four possible combinations of the letters on a piece of paper and then search the list until we find a word we recognize. The first way may sound a bit risky, whereas the second seems to be logical and very systematic. Unfortunately, if we had a ten-letter word in anagram form there would be 3,628,800 possible combinations of the letters to go through and that would take a fairly long time to work out.

One of the advantages of living in the last part of the twentieth century is that there are computers which can solve complicated problems like this very fast indeed. A computer will not necessarily be able to give you the final answer, but will produce a range of possible answers from which you must make your choice.

Often, though, the computer is either unavailable or not yet capable of processing the information. John Brown's immediate problem was not the sort that could be handled by a machine, it needed his brain; either he could try to develop a systematic, logical approach (sometimes called a scientific or deductive method), or he could let his mind explore the problem in a random fashion. This kind of approach has been called 'lateral thinking'* and can be very useful in this kind of situation.

* See *Lateral Thinking for Management* by Edward de Bono (McGraw-Hill, 1971).

Ask and it shall be given you

In looking for possible solutions to problems, remember two other things. First, someone else may well have faced the problem and can remember how he solved it. Second, people are often willing to give advice (especially when they have no responsibility for taking the decision). The role of adviser is well-established and still common in government circles. As a manager you can rely on your own skill, knowledge and experience (including what you have read about others in the same situation) or you can ask for advice. Either way you are still responsible for the decision in the end.

4 Evaluate the possibles

This stage of decision-making is a bit like a filtering process: gradually eliminating options until only two or three are left. The first thing is to get rid of obviously unsuitable possibilities.

Spring Clamps (2): the likely alternatives

John Brown wrote down some ideas on a piece of paper in an attempt to solve the problem of the lack of spring clamps. By 12.50 he had seven possibilities. They were:

1 Do nothing.
2 Phone his own boss.
3 Phone Fred Smith's boss.
4 Phone Fred Smith's assistant again.
5 Phone someone else at Spring Clamps.
6 Drive over to Spring Clamps.
7 Send out a search party for Fred.

To do nothing would probably prove to be a bad mistake in the circumstances. Presumably by doing nothing, the hope would be that the assistant would use his initiative and send some more clamps, or that Fred would soon return. Both possibilities cannot be relied on, so ignore this option.

To drive over to Spring Clamps (number 6) would achieve little; it was twenty miles away and even with a motorway running from door to door there would hardly be enough time to go there, find someone, obtain enough clamps for the rest of the day and get back before 2 p.m.

Option 7, to send out a search party, would be fun but pointless.

This preliminary screening reduces the options to four. Each involves making a telephone call. One way of reducing the alternatives still further would be to ask the question: Which call is most likely to lead to the fastest delivery of clamps? The answer to this is that it could be any of the people at Spring Clamps. Phoning his own boss would do little good, partly because he too might be at lunch, partly because if he were available he would then have to phone Spring Clamps, and partly because it would reflect adversely on John Brown's own administrative set-up.

The filtering process reduces the options to three all of them involving a phone call to Spring Clamps. The question then is, which of these individuals at Spring Clamps should he choose to phone? We are not told enough about the relationship John Brown has with other people at that firm, but it seems obvious that he is most likely to ask himself: Who else do I know, who would do me a favour and who has the power to take action? He may also build in a condition, especially if he is particularly friendly with Fred and does not want to lose that friendship, namely: Which phone call is least likely to harm Fred?

At this point in the filtering process, the questions about each alternative must be relevant and must also help in arriving at a decision. In effect you are keeping a scorecard of each option and the answer to each question will add to, or subtract from, each alternative's overall score. As we will see in Chapter 11, if the alternatives can be stated in number form it is much easier to arrive at a decision.

The difficulty in making this decision is the fact that John Brown cannot be certain that the forecasts will turn out according to the calculations. In other words there is an element of risk and this applies to all decisions: we can never be sure about the future and this is what makes many decisions difficult.

Probables, possibles and unlikelies Sometimes we can use numbers to help obtain better forecasts and reduce the uncertainty a little; this will also be studied in Chapter 11. However, there are many situations where every manager has to rely on his own judgement. In other words the alternatives have to be put on to a kind of scale, like this:

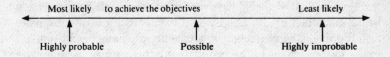

5 Take the decision

All of us are taking decisions all of the time. Generally we are not even conscious of doing so because we do not need to evaluate the alternatives each time. We have established for ourselves rules or policies which steer us in one direction or another. These kinds of decisions need to be taken once only consciously; thereafter they become rules and our actions in future are geared to these rules. This type of decision has been described as a 'programmed' decision – it is routine, repetitive and subject to established policies.

A non-programmed decision, on the other hand, is the kind of decision that causes most difficulty. However, if the preceding steps have been taken seriously, then often the decision itself is not difficult to make: it becomes obvious which course of action to take because of the process of elimination that you have already undertaken. Peter Drucker has described the Japanese decision-making process as one which focuses not on giving the answer, but on defining the question.* Even so the decision has to be reached. It may be perfectly obvious which course of action is the best, but there is often some hesitation before 'pressing the button'.

It has been said that the successful decision-maker has to have courage, and indeed in conditions of great uncertainty where the decision will affect many people, the need to act courageously is essential. The decision of General Eisenhower during the Second World War to go ahead with the D-Day invasion of continental Europe required a great deal of courage, for example.

* *Management*, pp. 374–9.

Most managerial decisions are not nearly so far-reaching in their effects, yet a degree of courage is required for all but the simplest. Indecision comes not only from being unable to decide on the most likely results, but also from fear of the consequences – for example, if the result of the decision is to be extremely unpopular. Generally, however, it is surprising how little reaction there is to most decisions, and if people have been involved in the earlier stages of the problem-solving activity there will be even less reaction (see Drucker on Japanese decision-making here too). Indecision and uncertainty often upset people more than an adverse decision.

Finally, it is as well to remember that when dealing with people it is impossible to please everyone all of the time. In fact, there are occasions when a few have to suffer in order that the majority may benefit. If this kind of situation appears, then you must not avoid the decision. Similarly there are times when a decision which may lead to long-term benefits causes short-term difficulties.

6 Implement the decision

Implementation turns the decision into action; it is the step that makes something actually happen. At a simple level, we may look at a crossword puzzle clue and when we think we have solved the problem we take a decision; but only when the answer is written down is the task completed.

In the same way, a managerial decision either has to be acted on by the manager himself or he has to communicate it to others for action. I will be looking at the importance of communications in Chapter 10, but there is another implication; a decision often means a change and that, as we shall see in the next chapter, may need handling with care.

John Brown at Spring Clamps took the decision to phone Fred Smith's assistant. Obviously that, on its own, was insufficient; John had to get on the phone and talk to the assistant. He did so and it was only a matter of minutes before a supply of clamps was *en route* for John's works.

Get the timing right   Whenever you make a managerial decision you can either implement it immediately – if, for example, it is urgent – or you may decide to keep the decision private for a while. There are good reasons for taking this second course of action and they include situations where some preparatory work has to be carried out first. For instance, a company may decide to buy a plot of land but first it will need to make some inquiries as to the ownership of the land, likely cost and also ensure that adequate finance is available. A premature announcement would possibly drive up the price or result in a competitive bid.

Equally inappropriate is the decision that is implemented too late – or at the eleventh hour. There is possibly nothing more annoying than having to rush through arrangements for some event because the decision was not made known until very late in the day. An essential ingredient in the planning process is the allowance of adequate time between the decision and the event itself. Generally the rule should be that the more complex the event, the longer the time for preparation.

Two views of decision-making

One writer on the subject of decision-making who warrants a special mention is H. A. Simon. He considers that there are two distinct views of man as a decision-maker. The first, a 'classical' view, is that people have the following decision-making characteristics:

- completely rational;
- perfect knowledge about the problem;
- unconflicting objectives;
- a clear view of the alternatives;
- seeking an acceptable solution.

In contrast, Simon has suggested a 'behavioural model' which sees the manager overcoming problems in a much less idealized way, often by compromise, by muddling through, by not developing long-term plans. Certainly he will not be completely rational and will not have perfect knowledge. What we are faced with is the difference between what should happen and what often does take place.

Many decisions appear to be taken irrationally because they are taken under pressure; because the manager has not had sufficient time to think the problem through and evaluate all the alternatives properly. This kind of situation cannot be entirely avoided, but the frequency of such events can be diminished:

- by proper, careful planning;
- by establishing good, comprehensive (yet flexible) decision rules; and
- by thinking ahead.

The last activity is mainly one of anticipation. In other words, to avoid having to take hasty decisions try to anticipate what might happen, as we noted in relation to strategic planning.

Chester Barnard wrote in 1938 that in 'the fine art' of decision-making there are four situations to avoid:

1 Do not take decisions that are not pertinent.
2 Do not make a decision too early.
3 Do not make a decision you cannot do anything about.
4 Do not make a decision somebody else should make.

We have already noted that organizations have to change because their environment is changing, and it should now be clear that failing to change will sooner or later be disastrous. We have also looked at the way in which systematic planning can help an organization to adjust to the new set of circumstances continually being created by the world outside. However, a number of questions still need to be resolved about this notion of change, such as:

- *Where does change come from?*
- *What is its effect on individuals as well as organizations?*
- *Why is there often resistance to it?*
- *How should this resistance be handled?*
- *How can organizations make changes work?*

Each of these questions needs to be examined in some detail if we are to appreciate properly the nature of change and how to manage it.

Where does change come from?

Changes may be classified in the following ways:

- those that occur within the organization *v.* those originating outside in the environment;
- those that can be controlled *v.* those that cannot be managed or controlled directly.

Changes starting inside the organization

Some changes inside organizations occur naturally and cannot be controlled. People, machinery and buildings get older day by day and this process cannot be prevented. Other changes may be controlled to some extent, such as the rate at which people leave the organization, the number of accidents that occur or the frequency with which equipment is replaced.

Other changes that emanate from within organizations are those that are deliberately started (apart from those resulting from necessity). People inside organizations change things for all kinds of reasons, sometimes unnecessary. Most of us have come across motor car 'tinkerers': people who love adjusting, fine-tuning and playing with their cars generally. In exactly the same way, some people within organizations are for ever tinkering with the system, simply because they are always conscious of the inefficiency of things.

Generally, however, changes are introduced because someone inside the business is dissatisfied with the status quo. This may be the result of an individual's own thinking or, quite possibly, some committee decision. A manager on his own may decide not to change anything; however, working in concert with a group, he may well have the courage to take a 'change' decision. The term 'change agent' is used to refer either to the individual, or to the group which instigates a change.

Changes starting in the environment

We have seen how the environment is changing in many different ways and also how different environments can affect organizations. It is possible to consider four kinds of environmental change:

- Irrelevant changes – those which are unlikely to affect the organization. For example, a revolution in South America will not affect your local pub's trade.
- Changes available for invitation – those which will affect the organization only if it chooses to get involved. Every organization has the choice of using a new technology or ignoring it. Similarly, a revolution in South America may lead to a decision by an exporting organization to open up a market in that particular country.

- Changes which can be prevented – those that will affect the organization unless it takes evasive action or counter-measures. This occurs where a rival company brings out a competitive product; unless something is done to offset the impact of the new product, there could be a drop in the company's market share.
- Changes which cannot be prevented. This class includes legislation and social trends.

It should also be noted that very large or powerful organizations may actually be able to influence their environments to some extent and thus protect themselves against adverse changes. Just how far this is possible is open to speculation.

What is the effect of change on individuals? How do they respond to it?

A case for consideration

Axelrod Grime ran a small fleet of taxis and was fairly successful at it. There came the point, however, when he had to change the cars he was using for new ones. He decided on the model of car he wanted and on all the other optional features that the manufacturer was offering. The only thing that posed a problem for him was deciding whether or not to have automatic gear-boxes fitted.

He calculated that the extra cost of fuel that results from using an automatic gear-box is less than the cost of repairing the car's clutch and the consequent loss of profit because the taxi is off the road. However, the problem that was holding him up was that he did not know how receptive or unreceptive his drivers would be to the idea of automatic gears. He himself wanted the change: would the drivers? He decided to ask them for their views one day after lunch.

The reactions were mixed: some were completely indifferent, but in most the announcement provoked a fairly strong response. There were those who considered that a car without a manual gear-box is not a car at all and said they would never drive such a vehicle. At the other extreme were those who felt that an automatic gear-box makes driving so much easier and less tiring that they would never do without it.

Once again we have a continuum of attitudes ranging from the extremely favourable to the downright hostile (see the diagram below). Some will be pleased, some annoyed, some upset – and this kind of mixed reaction is likely to occur whenever a change is suggested in all kinds of situations. In addition there is the individual who thought of the idea in the first place – the generator of the change.

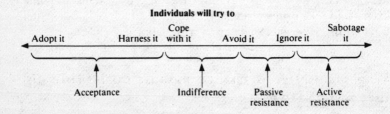

In their attitudes towards change, therefore, people can be classified into a number of categories. But we should remember that individuals do not fall exclusively into one category or another; a person may demonstrate considerable hostility towards one new development inside an organization and at the same time welcome or even initiate some other change. It would seem, though, that individuals tend to lean more towards one category than another.

People who initiate change

These are the individuals who have bright ideas, who suggest different ways of doing things, who seem never to be content with the status quo and are not satisfied with the way the future prospects of the organization appear to be shaping up. They range from the original thinkers of history, the inventors and the revolutionaries, to businessmen, entrepreneurs, politicans (of all parties) and research scientists.

Business organizations typically start up with an individual who has a bright idea, and it is not uncommon to find that companies with innovators at their head are continually changing – their products, markets, structure and ways of operating.

As organizations grow and the original entrepreneurs retire, so this type of individual is less and less popular because of his tendency to rock the boat. Yet there is always a need for the innovator because his ideas of today may well create the things which will save the company tomorrow. Successful organizations have strong teams in the marketing and design functions and – where there is manufacturing – in research and product development.

In the public services it is often said that there is no room at all for the innovator, and that bureaucracies develop only in size and as a means of protecting the existing state of affairs. Given that the work of public institutions is clearly established, it is obvious that fundamental changes in – for example – levels of service cannot be made. However, many internal changes can be made in these organizations such as in the efficiency of the systems that are being used. Without some innovators in the public service there would be no computers in use and no electric light in offices, while wearing bowler-hats would be compulsory.

People who accept change

People who accept change are found in all walks of life. At one extreme these are the individuals who were the first to have pocket calculators and video-cassette recorders at home. At work, they are the people who are continually pushing for new equipment or new facilities. Such people take a creative idea, encourage it and develop it. In this sense they are the true 'agents of change', responsible for making sure that ideas get implemented. They are undoubtedly a great asset in any organization that needs to make changes, because their enthusiasm for the new ideas can carry along the more reluctant members of the group.

On the other hand, to have too many enthusiastic adopters of ideas about could fairly quickly result in a haphazard organization, with new ideas being developed before the old ones had had time to settle down and make a contribution.

Another type within the general category of acceptance is the people who simply accept change and harness it for their own use. These are the individuals who quietly take the new development into their own area of influence and make sure that it works.

People who tend to be indifferent to change

This classic attitude towards change is best described in the expression 'So what?' Many changes within organizations are met with indifference, even apathy, especially if the people concerned perceive that their own overall state will remain the same. Such people learn to cope with the change when it arrives ('We can live with it'); or will try to avoid it as long as they possibly can.

The danger in this kind of attitude is the assumption – the perception – that their own state will be unchanged. This is a particularly dangerous assumption for a group of people to make – especially at senior management level – with regard to changes that are taking place outside the organization.

People who resist change

People who resist change may do so either passively or actively. Passive resistance will include those who will not learn about new ideas or who will do everything to avoid having to contend with something different. Old ladies do not take readily to pocket calculators, and old-fashioned organizations try to avoid or ignore the implications of microprocessors.

At the extreme end of the spectrum there are the actively hostile resisters. These individuals will be expressing their resistance in such activities as a 'go-slow', strikes, 'spoiling' products, or even acts of deliberate sabotage – thus perpetuating a tradition started by the Luddites in 1812 when they smashed up textile machinery.

The range of responses to change I have described can be called 'behavioural effects', because they are alterations in the way in which people carry out their work. We should remember that there may also be psychological effects – where a change is so dramatic that it causes a mental disturbance – and physiological effects, where the person concerned becomes physically ill. Alvin

Toffler, in his book *Future Shock*,* gives many examples of the effects of change. He quotes some research which showed that individuals who have experienced a dramatic change in their lives are more likely to be ill than people whose lives are more stable. Similarly, techniques recently developed by the British Safety Council show that accidents at work are often connected with high levels of stress – stress itself being caused by significant changes in personal circumstances such as divorce, death of a spouse and even giving up smoking.

Why are there different attitudes to change?

In the case of the taxi firm, it was suggested that the individual drivers would differ: some would welcome change, some would resist it and some would be indifferent. It is easy to label such reactions as 'dangerous radical', 'dogmatic conservative' and 'lazy apathetic', but this is neither helpful nor particularly accurate. Many factors have been proposed which might account for a particular individual's attitude towards a change, and any manager wishing to make a change should be aware of such underlying influences. Some of these are:

General attitude towards change This is something to do with personality that makes for either a general resistance to, or acceptance of, changes.

Cultural values and beliefs Individuals, organizations and groups build up their own value systems, codes of conduct or behaviour, and a change which in any way runs counter to these is likely to be met with stiff resistance. At a simple level, it may be accepted practice to stop work a little early on Friday afternoon – and good luck to the new manager who attempts to change that! At a much more significant level are efforts to get people to do things which are contrary to their moral or religious beliefs.

Feelings of insecurity These are also personality traits and often result in strong opposition to change, even though this may be quite irrational.

* Published by Pan Books, 1971.

Relationship with organization/leader   Where an individual has a high regard for the organization in which he is working, and especially for his boss, his attitude is going to be different from that of the person who trusts neither his boss nor the organization.

The pattern of past events   Individuals evaluate changes that affect them by looking for similar occurrences in the past. 'Last time they did that, it was a disaster' is the kind of statement made about a prospective change, and is to be head quite frequently in politics about an opposing political party's views. The alternative belief from a supporter is, 'Last time our people did this, it was a great success.'

Why is there resistance to change?

It has been said that people do not resist change itself. What they are resisting is the implication behind the change (whether real or imagined) that somehow they are going to be harmed. This harm may be one or a combination of various factors, including:

Economic   If a change is perceived as likely to affect the money in the pocket, or the amount of work required to produce the same money, then it will probably be resisted. One of the problem areas in recent years has been the question of new technology and its impact on individuals. While people may clearly understand how increasing productivity (through the use of more technology) can raise wages, there is still resistance because of the fear of losing jobs.

Inconvenience   Resistance to change may be greater if it seems as though it will make life more difficult. This often occurs when offices or factories are moved from one place to another. The Location of Offices Bureau, which used to have the responsibility of encouraging firms to move out of London, could demonstrate the economic and social advantages without too much difficulty. Even so, many firms would not move because of the perceived inconvenience of being away from the capital.

Freedom   An individual will resist an idea if he feels that his freedom is going to be diminished by it. For instance, trying to introduce clocking-in and clocking-out into an organization which has never known such procedures would have very little chance of success; it would be like trying to move from McGregor's Theory Y back to Theory X (see p. 57). Greater control may be desirable in certain circumstances, but that may not be how the individuals who are going to be controlled will see it.

Security   If a proposed change suggests that there may be a threat to the security of jobs, then it is likely that there will be some resistance to it. Once again this may be an imagined rather than a likely outcome, but it will affect the behaviour of individuals nonetheless.

Estimating resistance

As a manager planning to make a change, you should first of all try to assess the extent to which this change might be resisted. One man with significant involvement in this kind of work is Kurt Lewin. He developed the technique called 'force-field analysis', which is a useful way of identifying on one hand, the resisting elements in an organization, and on the other the forces in favour of the change. The technique is specific to any one change, the 'forces' being different for each change that is proposed.

The technique also shows the relative strength or weakness of each element in the equation, and is often expressed in the form of a diagram (see below). The diagram illustrates clearly how the driving forces that are seeking to achieve a change come up

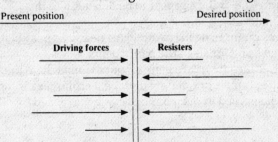

against a number of restraining or resisting factors. The relative strengths of the driving forces and of the resisters are indicated by the length of the arrows. In order to achieve the desired objective, either the driving forces have to be strengthened (which can lead to more conflict) or else attempts have to be made to reduce the strength of the resistance (or remove it altogether).

Reducing resistance to change

There are many ways in which any individual or group can express resistance to a planned change. You will have seen films where A is trying to persuade B to change or do something he or she does not want to do! Normally the manager does not have to go so far as to get down on his bended knees and plead with his subordinates to change. On the other hand, it is unlikely that he will revert to the method used by the owner of a small company who reputedly called his staff together and said, 'Now, look, it's time you changed your attitudes.'

Amongst the more sensible approaches are these:

- The change should have the full support and commitment of senior management.
- The change is more acceptable if the ideas come from the team that has to change and it is a group decision based on a group diagnosis.
- It helps if the change appears to reduce work-loads.
- The change should not threaten livelihoods or income.
- Changes that sound interesting and exciting will meet less resistance, i.e. if they appear to be of benefit to the participants.
- Changes ought to be in harmony (as nearly as possible) with the values and ideals of the participants.
- Economic incentives are helpful, but mainly where the resistance is on economic grounds. An economic incentive may not succeed in overcoming resistance caused by other fears.

Making change work

We have seen that change in an organization is either the result of some outside event which imposes its effect on the organization, or else it comes from within the organization. Some internal changes cannot be planned (such as the sudden death of a key manager), although their impact can be lessened by perceptive planning. However, the majority of internal changes are the result of a decision taken by an individual or by a group, and it is these that need most attention. As Chester Barnard pointed out, there is absolutely no point in deciding to change something if the change cannot be made effective.

Force-field analysis provides information as to the likely extent to which resistance will be felt, but even if the resisting factors are reduced there is no guarantee that the decision will be successfully implemented unless a number of other steps are taken:

Keep people informed It is easy to inform people of a decision to make a change, and just as easy to tell them of the reasons for the decisions. Keeping people in the dark encourages rumour and speculation.

Get the group involved In Chapter 5 I introduced 'leadership continuum', which ranged from the autocratic to the democratic. Group decision-making is a useful way of introducing change because it increases the commitment and interest of the members of the team, and is likely to be effective more quickly. You should, however, bear in mind the qualifying points made in Chapter 5: that a sudden switch in leadership style will be viewed with suspicion; that unless the group is qualified and willing, it may not be able to take proper action.

Group involvement is not a recipe for the successful introduction of a change in all circumstances, although it is always useful to obtain the group's reaction to an idea.

Reversible changes On occasions it may be possible to introduce a change on a provisional basis, making it clear to all concerned that the idea is experimental and is to run for a limited period of time. There is a lot to be said in favour of a pilot scheme if such a scheme will provide answers to questions which are needed for a permanent decision. Experimental systems and pilot schemes also enable everyone concerned to get a feel for the new proposal. On the other hand, a pilot scheme can be very expensive and the delay in taking the decision to go the whole way may spoil the chances of ultimate success.

All changes are capable of being reversed in the long run, but the cost of returning to the old situation may be very high in terms of both money and personal inconvenience – as it would be if computers were introduced for a limited period of time. In making the change, therefore, it is worth spelling out the extent to which it is reversible.

Fast or slow change? Slow change is often recommended because it is less disruptive than rapid change. Taking things a step at a time is commendable where a great deal of retraining is needed, or where resources cannot match the requirements of a full, comprehensive launch. This might occur, for instance, where a company wants to introduce a new revolutionary product throughout Europe. The cost of training all the sales-people and providing adequate promotional support is very high, so it may have to be introduced in gradual stages. In addition, slow change is worth considering where you need to get the individuals involved used to an idea – especially where it is unlikely to have been experienced before. For instance, someone who has always used a gas cooker needs time to become familiar with an electric cooker.

The disadvantage of slow change is that by moving slowly the opportunity may pass without your being able to take full advantage of it; moreover, it is possible that by the time the change is fully implemented the new system is already out of date and inappropriate. Nowhere is this problem more acute than in the case of technological change; an airline which gradually replaces its planes finds that by the time it has replaced all its machines a completely new generation of aircraft is on the market: the firm is now flying brand-new, obsolete planes.

Finally, changing something quickly has the advantage of reducing uncertainty: the state of not knowing what is going to happen is one of the causes of stress.

How much change?   Some organizations exist in relatively stable environments. A hospital, for instance, need not change and adapt too much because the environment in which it is operating does not alter too much from year to year. Changes that it makes are mainly by way of improvement rather than being of major strategic importance. Other organizations exist in turbulent environments, where the future is unpredictable and where the way the firm operates (its system) may need to be changed frequently – such as in computer and communications technologies.

Change made simply for the sake of it is not often a good rule. On the other hand, failing to change at all is equally dangerous. An inflexible manager, group or organization is at risk from the changing environment just as surely as the dinosaurs were when they failed to adapt to theirs.

There are therefore two elements in the answer to the question: How much change? Namely:

■ the speed and size of change in the environment; and
■ the flexibility and readiness to change of the individuals within the organization.

Training   Where your organization needs to change but the individuals within it do not have the flexibility or willingness to do so, then there is a problem, since your attempts at change will be resisted. Short-run solutions may be effective for minor changes, but in order to achieve a fully flexible, forward-looking organization individuals will have to be trained to be more adaptable and forward-looking likewise. It has been suggested that 'organizations need to provide the appropriate climate to allow managerial growth and the development of change-responsive managers'.*

Change that hurts   Inevitably there are times when you will have to make changes that cause problems for individuals. At worst there is the difficult decision to fire someone because of his unsuitability or because his services are no longer needed. You can't avoid these changes, but you can sometimes soften their impact by the

* D. C. Basil and I. Cook, *The Management of Change*, McGraw-Hill, 1974.

way in which you communicate the decision. A swift announcement given openly and with appropriate compensation is better than an ill-timed decision communicated by hearsay or signs.

Managing the transition Sometimes a change is so great that it takes a lot of time and effort to implement. In these situations it is useful to appoint a transition team, which is responsible for making sure that the change takes place with the minimum fuss and bother. Sometimes such a team consists of outsiders (or even a single consultant), but often it is drawn from key personnel within the organization who fall into the category of enthusiastic adoptors (discussed on p. 85). The team should consist of individuals representing all the different levels and functions that will be affected by the change, so that no group of individuals is left unrepresented.

Planned change (as opposed to natural change) is therefore an important managerial function. All managers must spend some time deliberately thinking about making changes and then actively causing these changes to take place. The key steps can be summarized as follows:

1 *Develop a concern* Ask questions such as: Could we do it better? Do we need to change anything? Will we need to change things tomorrow?
2 *Share the concern* Involve others in answering the questions.
3 *Define and solve the problems* What should we do that is new?
4 *Recognize the effects of change on individuals.*
5 *Assess capability* Make sure the organization and the individuals can cope with the proposed changes.
6 *Train* Individuals may have to learn to cope with an increasing amount of change.
7 *Implement.*

8 Time Management

C. Northcote Parkinson, in his famous book *Parkinson's Law*, tells the story of the old lady who has to write a postcard to her niece:

An elderly lady of leisure can spend the entire day in writing and dispatching a postcard to her niece at Bognor Regis. An hour will be spent in finding the postcard, another in hunting for spectacles, half an hour in a search for the address, an hour and a quarter in composition, and twenty minutes in deciding whether or not to take an umbrella when going to the pillar-box in the next street. The total effort that would occupy a busy man for three minutes all told may in this fashion leave another person prostrate after a day of doubt, anxiety and toil.

Parkinson's thesis was that the more time you have available to do a job, the longer it will take. 'Work expands,' he said, 'to fill the time available.'

Unfortunately, many managers reading this tend to reply: 'That may be a correct analysis for old ladies of leisure, but it certainly does not apply to me. I work damned hard, I cut corners, things do not get done, yet still there aren't enough hours in the day.'

It is quite likely that you have heard the expression, 'I don't have enough time', or something similar within the last few days. This is in regular use, whether as an excuse for failing to do something or as a way of getting out of doing something altogether. There are busy people whose day seems to be action-packed – who never rest, whose work-load seems over-full and who often say, 'Sorry, I just have not had the time to deal with it.' Yet there are other busy people who also have action-packed days, who never rest and whose work-load seems over-full; nevertheless, these people always do things on time and even have spare time to deal with extra emergency jobs.

The truth is that time is the only factor that you can do absolutely nothing to increase. You can increase your skills and knowledge; your experience grows with the passage of time; you can foster and develop your personal relationships. But you cannot increase the amount of time you have; it is strictly limited. Admittedly, there are a few individuals who need only a little sleep and who actually find an extra hour or two each day to do things, but for most people there can be no difference at all in the time available. Some people achieve more each day than others – a few because they have more energy than the rest, and some because they have more to do, but most because they manage their time effectively. Or to be more accurate, they manage their work-loads more efficiently within the time available.

Therefore, instead of wasting time complaining about the lack of it, it is worth spending some time trying to organize things so that there is enough time available.

The first question to ask is: What wastes your time?

There are, of course, various answers to this question. Outside work hours many people rank television as a major time-consumer. However, in a work environment many reply that it is their boss who is the greatest time-waster. Some consider that meetings are the main culprit, others are convinced that the abolition of the telephone would solve all their problems. Unfortunately, answers like these may well be missing the point: why worry about spending time in ways over which one has no control? What you have to discover is where time can be saved by a conscious effort on your part. The easiest way of doing this is to look at the major supposed causes of wasted time and see what scope exists for spending less time on them. (Meetings will be considered separately in Chapter 9.)

Travelling

In most organizations the sales personnel do the most travelling, and the biggest complaint made by the majority of sales managers is that they spend too much time in this way. Certainly a very high percentage of their time *is* spent on the road – presumably visiting clients who cannot be handled by the ordinary salesman, or calling on individual sales personnel in their own territory. Leaving aside the argument that many people prefer to be out and about rather than sitting at a desk in the office, the main reason for travelling is to carry out some discussion which cannot be conducted by telephone. Among such discussions are:

- training subordinates if they are located in different places;
- where it is necessary to discuss complicated documents with others (e.g. discussing architect's drawings on the phone is a tricky and even dangerous activity);
- where a face-to-face discussion is more appropriate and has to be on the client's home ground.

The difficulty here is to decide what is appropriate. For instance, if a customer has a complaint it may be handled by telephone, but the sales manager may feel that a face-to-face discussion will clear the air more effectively. Similarly, within an organization which has a number of locations some individuals spend a good deal of time visiting all the 'outposts of the empire'. These visits may be simply a public relations activity to make each branch or depot feel part of a planning or control process.

Travelling is therefore an essential ingredient in many managers' work-loads. We need to ask: Is it possible to reduce the amount of time spent in transit over the year? In order to answer this you can put the following supplementary questions:

- Is my journey really necessary? What would happen if I did not go – for instance, because I was ill?
- Why would a telephone conversation be insufficient?
- Is it possible to combine two or more visits and make one long trip? (This needs just a little more planning.)
- Why can a subordinate not make the journey instead of me? Many visits are made because an assistant is considered to have insufficient expertise to handle the discussion successfully. The answer here is to make sure that your assistants are trained to take this kind of responsibility. Again you can ask: What happens if I fall ill?
- Am I taking the quickest route and mode of transport?

And finally, on a completely different level:

■ Am I based in the best place so as to minimize overall
   travelling time?

The above discussion has been related to travelling away from the
place of work, but to a lesser extent it also applies within the
work-place, especially if this is a large organization. An enormous amount of time can be wasted walking from office to office,
especially if there is a danger of many social meetings in the
corridors. The six questions posed above are as relevant for
journeys within the work-place as for those outside..

Doing other people's work

Very few people admit to doing work which does not strictly
concern them and which should be done by someone else; yet it
happens all the time. In Chapter 6 on decision-making and
problem-solving, one question that was posed very early on was:
Is this really my problem, or is it just someone passing the buck?
Too often a manager finds himself getting involved in something
that he need not be concerned about; he becomes a vacuum-
cleaner sucking in all manner of jobs, all kinds of work – much of
which should have nothing to do with him. There are three main
ways in which this can crop up.

First, there is the request for help from a colleague. Normally a
manager has a particular expertise which is available to other
managers as part of the everyday running of the organization.
There is obviously no suggestion that the manager should abro-
gate his responsibilities and deny his colleagues technical assistance, but there are times when the request is not for technical
help but merely for moral support. 'Have a look at this, George,
and tell me what you think of it'; this approach is not entirely
unknown and George, if he is not careful, finds himself reading
reports that do not really concern him and over which he has no
influence and no control.

Second, a subordinate may come to his boss with a problem. If
he is smart, he can pass the problem to his boss without the latter

having recognized what is happening. This is often achieved by the use of some subtle flattery: 'You solved it so well last time. How did you do it?' It is often easier to deal with the matter yourself than to coach a subordinate to do so, and so the job changes hands.

The third way of acquiring more work than you need is by failing to pass it on to the person who should deal with it – in other words, by not delegating work. There are several reasons why you might fail to delegate:

- your subordinate is not competent or trustworthy;
- your subordinate says he is too busy;
- your subordinate will kick up a fuss;
- you enjoy doing that particular job yourself ('We have to visit these ten organizations; you take the ones in London, Glasgow, Birmingham and Manchester. I suppose I ought to visit the one in Paris.').

Occasionally you may find that any of the first three are valid reasons for not delegating; however, part of your job is to make sure that your subordinates are ready, willing and able to take on work.

The important thing about delegation is that it is a sign of strength in a manager, not a weakness. To be effective, it embraces four particular aspects:

- passing out the job to the subordinate;
- giving him the authority to do everything needed to complete the job;
- making him responsible for the successful completion of the job;
- rewarding him adequately.

The manager must also ensure that the job to be done is properly understood by the subordinate.

As far as doing things you enjoy is concerned, it is occasionally fair enough to take on something particularly enjoyable or interesting. However, too much of this practice demotivates subordinates, especially if your reasons for doing so are not entirely honest.

Remember that delegation means passing on good things as well as not-so-good things.

The ditherer

One of the most difficult time-wasters to pin down is the manager who is indecisive. Often he can be recognized because he is the one who is either continually asking for more information on a problem, or who goes over the same ground several times. To be dependent on such people for a decision is exceedingly frustrating, and is best countered by a fairly unequivocal statement to the effect that, 'I would like a decision by Friday, otherwise I shall go ahead and paint it yellow.' In this way you can be sure of provoking a response within the time limit.

The chatterer

Chatting is a part of every manager's work; part of the process of getting on with the job, and an important aspect of developing good relationships. However, too much of it wastes time and it is a particularly difficult thing to cope with. Sometimes it has to be tolerated – like travelling – but if the chat is occasional, then you will have to put a stop to it after a reasonable time. If it is a face-to-face chat, then have an excuse ready – for example, that a meeting or a phone call is imminent. If it is a chatterer on the phone, then an excuse like, 'The boss has just walked in' or even, 'My desk has just caught fire' is a way of getting out of the difficulty.

The meddler

The meddler is someone who will not let subordinates get on with the job, but who continually interferes. Benign meddlers are those who like to help 'to speed things up', but in fact are really slowing things down. There is also the suspicious meddler, whose idea of control is to breathe down people's necks and watch their every move. These people may have to be tolerated, but they may – occasionally and politely – be asked to go away.

Doing it yourself

A good way of wasting time is to try to do everything yourself, rather than to call in experts. This is important in relation to problem-solving, where a manager may spend a good deal of time and effort trying to work out the solution when all he needs to do is make a quick telephone call to an expert and get the answer in seconds.

The elegant solution

There are some people who will go to extraordinary lengths to solve a problem when only a quick, simple answer is required. To this kind of person, the interest lies not in the solution but in the problem itself. There will be examples of this in all organizations: the fifty-page report containing complicated diagrams and charts to explain why the cost of fuel went up by 10%; the expensive piece of equipment to solve a simple problem (e.g. the electronic fly-swat). This kind of approach has its place, and such people are valuable in those circumstances which require a high degree of precision and care. It is up to you as the manager of such individuals to make sure that they understand precisely the level of detail required, and that their efforts are focused on problems that need painstaking skill. If a problem can be solved by a quick calculation on the back of an envelope, ask someone who is good at that kind of thing.

Paper, paper everywhere

Most managers have to deal with quite a lot of paperwork. If the documents are the result of a request by your manager, you should make sure that they are all as brief as possible. If you are in a position to state how much information you would like to receive, then you must let it be known and normally should err on the side of brevity. I will look at this in more detail in Chapter 10 on communications.

Just as long reports are time-wasters, so too is a large proportion of the unsolicited paper that a manager receives. If this is not dealt with fairly quickly, it can soon build up into monster piles under which he finally becomes buried. There are only three things to be done with paper:

- throw it away;
- file it;
- do something with it.

Some ideas on saving time

Handling the boss

In addition to the points already made with regard to boss/subordinate relationships, there are four extra things to note about handling the boss (assuming that he is aware of the subordinate's competence). Ask:

1 What does he want, precisely?
2 When does he want it?
3 In what form does he want it?

Then state:

4 Whether it can be done or not.

Just occasionally it may be necessary to say 'No' or 'Later' to a boss if there is a valid reason for doing so.

Using a secretary/assistant

A good secretary or personal assistant can save a lot of time if used as a secretary and not just as a shorthand-typist. For example, in Chapter 6 we considered the problem of the spring clamps. One of the apparent difficulties seemed to be that the young secretary failed to contact Fred Smith at Spring Clamps. Had she been given an explanation of the problem, it is possible she would have been more persistent in her efforts. A good secretary would have managed either to get through to either the right person or an acceptable substitute.

Among the other useful secretarial functions which save time are:

- blocking unwanted telephone or personal callers (especially if a meeting is in progress);
- planning timetables for travelling and meetings;
- keeping filing in order;
- acting as an information researcher and source.

Where it is not possible to have a secretary or an assistant, you will have to carry out many of these things yourself. In these circumstances it is useful to be on good terms with whoever does typing work (e.g. the typing pool), and also with the telephone-switchboard operators.

Discussion and interview control

A very high proportion of most managers' time is spent in talking to people both inside and outside meetings. Discussions, interviews or telephone conversations are usually on a one-to-one basis, or with just two or three people at most. To save time on these occasions:

- decide how long is needed to discuss the issue;
- tell the people involved how long it will take;
- make sure there will be no interruptions (if possible);
- decide and inform the relevant personnel as to the purpose of the interview etc.
- give adequate notice to all concerned.

Crisis avoidance

A crisis is an unplanned event which disrupts or threatens to disrupt normal operations. When a crisis occurs, it wastes a colossal amount of time – as we saw with the spring-clamps case.

Obviously, crises will occur in even the best-managed organizations, but all too often crisis management becomes a way of life rather than an exception. An organization which is likely to have major, completely unpredictable crises may create a permanent standing committee, consisting of a cross-section of senior managers who are called together in the event of a storm. Generally, though, a crisis is overcome by hard work and effort on the part of the individual managers who become involved.

Crisis avoidance is a preferable way of running an organization, and the purpose of control systems is to ensure that if things start to get out of hand, steps can be taken quickly so as to stop the problem from spreading. You will recall that one of the keys to successful control is the speed with which the system operates. Since the responsible manager is at the centre of the system, he must get the necessary information, reach a decision and act quickly to stop the crisis. If he is disorganized and not managing his time properly, then the crisis soon gets out of hand.

Work-load planning

The most effective managers are those who manage their time in such a way that the important things get priority. This needs thinking through, therefore a certain amount of time has to be invested at the outset. The key steps in this particular activity are:

- Decide how you should spend your time over a normal week. Establish priorities: give most time to the most important things. Bear in mind that at least fifteen per cent of working time is wasted for natural reasons; this is called the 'relaxation factor' by work-study experts.
- Find out how you actually spend your time by keeping a fairly detailed log over a four-week period.
- Look for obvious time-wasters and resolve to eliminate them.
- Set aside regular times for carrying out routine tasks like correspondence and reading any journals or magazines you should read.
- Allow adequate time for the unexpected.
- Give yourself some 'thinking time', especially before an interview or meeting.

- Maintain your time-log and use it as a basis for a personal time-control system.

Questions to ask continually from your time-log

- Am I doing anything that need not be done at all?
- Am I doing anything that should (or could) be done by someone else?
- Am I doing anything that wastes other people's time?
- Did I understand properly what I should do?
- Do other people understand properly what I need?
- How many time-wasting crises were my fault? How can I avoid a recurrence?
- Are the operating control systems efficient?

9 Meetings

Nearly everyone has some horror story to relate about a meeting that achieved nothing except a great deal of wasted time; it seems to happen all the while, yet nobody appears prepared to do anything about it. It is sometimes salutary to remember that time does have a price; for instance a meeting of six managers, each earning £15,000, costs £80 an hour. If every meeting had to produce benefits greater than the costs incurred during the meeting, the number of hours spent in this way would drop to one-tenth of their present level.

So why do meetings take place and what can be done to improve their effectiveness?

The purpose of meetings

Statutory

Many meetings are a legal requirement according to the constitution of the company, society or club concerned, and they usually fall into two (or three) sub-divisions:

The annual general meeting (AGM) This is the meeting of the members of the organization (shareholders in the case of a limited company). Normally these are fairly well-managed affairs, because the rules under which they operate are clearly set out in the organization's constitution. One of the most useful things to note about an AGM is that members have to be given plenty of advance notice of its occurrence, and must be provided with adequate information about the matters that are going to be discussed.

Meetings of officers Rules concerning the frequency of meetings of the elected or appointed officers are often written into the constitutions of organizations. This body of officers may be called the board of directors, the board of management, the council or the meeting of governors.

Since this kind of committee meeting is the senior one in any organization, there is usually a lot of business to get through. Only by efficient management can this be completed in time; once again, it is useful if the committee members receive adequate warning of meetings and have a good idea of the topics that will be discussed. In commercial undertakings it is usual for the members of the board of directors to have a monthly meeting at which the accounting results for the previous month are discussed. For a director to do his job properly, he needs to have the necessary information several days in advance, especially if he is expected to give an explanation or offer some help and advice. How can a director be helpful if he does not know the nature of the problem?

Meetings of executive officers Some organizations have written into their constitutions provision for regular meetings of the senior executives of the larger management committee. This may be an inner circle consisting of the chairman, secretary, treasurer (or other most senior financial manager) and the managing director (if a separate individual from the chairman). These three or four, whether legally obliged to do so or not, should have regular meetings to decide matters that do not need full committee approval, and also to make sure that full committee meetings are as efficient as possible.

In addition, if these executive officers are conscientious and fully devoted to the aims of the organizations they are serving, then the meetings should be used to develop a shared understanding of the prospects and problems of the firm: very much a think-tank or ideas laboratory at a very high level.

Meetings for dissemination of information

A completely different type of meeting is the kind which is called to spread information. This can best be achieved by a meeting if:

- there are many people to be informed;
- an element of persuasion is needed;
- something has to be shown or seen;
- the information is confidential;
- many questions are likely to be asked.

A good example of this is where a large company wants to tell its sales force about a new range of products. Calling them together is a much more effective way of spreading knowledge – and raising spirits.

Do bear in mind that meetings like this do not just 'happen'; a great deal of planning and management is involved if they are to be successful. If you wish to set up a large information-giving meeting of the kind just described, you must be absolutely sure you can afford to devote a great deal of time to it. If not, you should appoint professional conference organizers to handle the whole affair.

Smaller information-giving meetings need adequate planning too, and here there are three essential points to remember:

- tell people the subject matter of the meeting (as well as time, duration and place);
- prepare materials that people can see clearly, understand and take away with them;
- have a programme, tell everyone what it is and stick to it.

Problem-solving meetings

This kind of meeting is very common and arises because one individual does not have all the knowledge and information he needs in order to solve the problem on his own. Others are called in either because they have some specialist knowledge, or because the outcome of the meeting will affect their own operations in some way. However, there is a temptation to invite to such meetings too many individuals who have only a marginal contribution to make. It is better either to ask such people beforehand to stand by in case they are needed, or to ask for their opinion in advance. Too much time is wasted sitting in meetings, waiting to be asked to make a contribution that is only minor.

The other problem which crops up as a result of over-inviting is that the meeting takes longer. Remember Graicunas' theory of relationships in Chapter 3 (p. 28): the more people there are in a meeting, the greater the number of conversations that can be held. What could be solved by four people in twenty minutes would take six people two hours, while eight people would take five hours. Clearly in the interests of democracy and participation extra people have to be invited, but sometimes efficiency has to be sacrificed in the interests of democracy.

Once again, it is important to plan meetings like this adequately:

- give people as much notice as possible;
- tell them as precisely as possible what the problem is;
- inform them what might be expected of them;
- let them know who else will be there;
- tell them how long the meeting will be;
- give them any helpful documents and an agenda;
- make it clear that the decision will be yours alone and not a collective one.

Collective-decision meetings

Often meetings are used to get a collective decision from the members attending. If one individual does not have the power or authority to take the decision on his own, then a meeting will have to be called in order to do so. Sometimes those matters which have to be decided by a committee are laid down precisely in the organization's constitution. For example, in limited companies the auditors have to be appointed by the company AGM. Decisions about high finance – borrowing or raising new share capital – are often taken by boards of directors, or by AGMs on the recommendation of the directors.

The use of committees to make decisions is widespread – partly because it is felt that the decision is better if several people make it, and partly because of the fear of delegating too much power and authority to any one individual.

It is often the case that decisions are actually taken by the senior executive officer, but put to the full committee for ratification. This is a difficult path to tread, depending for its success on the degree of trust which the officer has built up with the committee.

However, there are occasions when any manager feels that to take a specific decision would be quite beyond his own authority, even though he may be absolutely convinced in his own mind as to what should be done.

There are also many occasions when you may be able to choose between taking the decision yourself and calling a meeting to decide. In these situations there are a number of factors which may affect the decision: How quickly does it have to be taken? How will my colleagues react? People naturally feel aggrieved if decisions which affect them are taken without their knowledge. What is worse is the situation where a decision only comes to the manager's notice via the informal communication system in the organization.

Finally, a meeting is sometimes called in order for a collective decision to be made, where the manager is not able to make up his own mind (even though he should). This is tantamount to an abdication of his responsibilities; he is saying, 'I am not capable of taking the decision'. This is perfectly acceptable occasionally, as long as it is done openly, but it can become a habit.

Creative thinking meetings

Sometimes meetings are called for the purpose of creativity: to try to come up with some new ideas. Creative thinking uses the idea of 'social facilitation', which is another way of describing what happens when a group of people get together to stimulate each other's thinking.

There are many different ways of tackling this kind of meeting. One such technique is known as 'brainstorming' and was developed by Alex Osborn in the early 1950s to help in coming up with new ideas in advertising, e.g. a new brand name for a product. In these sessions the problem is not actually stated beforehand, but clearly stated at the start. People are encouraged to produce as many ideas as possible. From these the best can be selected for further evaluation. Criticism is not allowed; the important thing is the development of the greatest possible number of ideas.

General tips for good creative thinking meetings   Have a mixed-knowledge group; male and female, if consumer goods are being considered. Between six and nine participants is ideal. Use a secretary to take notes, or a tape recorder. A blackboard or flip-chart is handy for posting up key words.

Brainstorming needs up to half an hour to be effective, but no more than one hour. Participants must know beforehand what kind of a meeting they will be attending, and what will be expected of them.

Other miscellaneous meetings

There are many other kinds of meeting: meetings to select new members of an organization; one-off meetings composed of neighbours wanting to fight a proposed new building, or managers wishing to fight an unwelcome change.

There are also psychological group activities such as T-groups and role-playing exercises which have specific behavioural objectives.

Making the most of meetings

Planning

I have already said enough about planning for it to be unnecessary to stress its general importance further. As far as meetings are concerned you need to consider the following:

■ Allow plenty of time.
■ Decide why the meeting is needed (if at all).
■ Decide when and where to hold it – the more notice you can give, the better.
■ Draw up an agenda:
■ Put financial statements (if any) first, because the state of

financial health may determine the outcome of other matters up for discussion;
- Put the most serious or urgent matters next;
- Make a timetable for the meeting;
- Clearly state what each item on the agenda involves. If it is an issue where there will be argument and discussion will finish with a vote, then it is better to put the item in the form of a proposal or motion. For instance: '*Item 4:* To consider and vote on the following resolution: "That this meeting agrees to move the company's operations to the Bahamas."' This is a more suitable form than: '*Item 4:* The move to the Bahamas.'
- Obtain any necessary reading matter and assemble it with the agenda.
- Decide who needs to attend, inform them well in advance and send them the full agenda with background papers.
- Tell those attending what they will be expected to do at the meeting (e.g. make a speech, present some information).

During the meeting

If you are going to be the chairman and have no previous experience, get some idea how others do it first. It is worth watching a really good chairman in action – the most easily available meeting to attend is one of the local council, though unfortunately there is no guarantee as to the quality of chairmanship there. However, such an occasion will provide good clues as to the effective conduct of meetings. The following points need to be remembered:

- Start on time.
- Stick to the timetable.
- Be fair.
- Give everyone a chance.
- Be prepared to shut someone up if they become over-talkative or repetitive.
- Make sure that people stick to the subject under discussion and that their remarks are relevant.
- State clearly which item is to be discussed.

- If a vote is needed, be sure that everyone is clear about what they are voting for.
- Allow only one person to talk at a time. If you expect a noisy meeting, get a gavel or a hammer and a block of wood; hitting the block may not stop the noise, but it relieves frustration.
- If action is needed as a result of a discussion, make sure it is clear who is to carry out the task and by what date.
- Make sure that decisions and significant statements are all fully recorded.
- Do not let the meeting drag on. (People tend to get tired after 1½ to 2 hours, after which mental agility falls rapidly; this is especially true of evening meetings.) It is better to halt the proceedings and arrange to continue at another time.

If you are a participant at a meeting, you should:

- Arrive on time.
- Come prepared.
- Listen.
- Avoid rambling discourses and repetition.
- If you have a strong view on something, make sure the meeting understands your view and why you hold it.

After the meeting

Make sure that minutes are prepared quickly and sent out to all who need to receive them. The minutes should state:

- what has been decided; and
- who is to take action.

Any person whose name appears in the minutes should have his or her attention drawn to the fact, so that the individual knows he has to take action.

The position of secretary

The special responsibilities of the inner circle of officers were mentioned on p. 107. The secretary has many administrative and legal duties, but is also responsible for much of the pre-planning which comes even before the rest of the inner circle become involved. In particular, it is the secretary who advises the chairman on how to handle the agenda, and he should also ensure that the chairman is fully briefed on the meeting. To this end, the preparation of the 'chairman's briefing paper' is invaluable, and the secretary should make sure that the chairman actually reads (and understands) it.

The contents of a briefing paper will vary, but generally it includes information about newcomers, meanings of technical terms that may be used and the legal position on matters which may arise, plus notes on any hostile attitudes that might appear.

A thoughtful secretary can save much time in meetings without having to do anything during the actual meeting to speed up the proceedings. After the meeting, he can expedite the implementation of decisions by making sure that things are happening – and helping to make them happen if there are problems.

Disadvantages of meetings

Apart from the obvious disadvantages that meetings can cost money and may waste time, there are two main dangers to guard against:

Meetings may lead to unsatisfactory compromise

It has been said that there are some things over which it is possible to compromise, and others where you should not do so. For example, in an argument over which of two small boys should eat an apple, it is possible to compromise nicely by cutting the apple in two. However, a similar compromise would not work if those two small boys were squabbling over a white rabbit! Meetings may end up by doing something similar to cutting the white rabbit in half, simply because they do not want to upset one of their members.

Meetings may be indecisive

It has also been said that if you do not want to have to take a decision, you should appoint a committee to inquire into the problem. Inevitably that committee will spawn a couple of sub-committees, and a further special committee will be created to coordinate the work of the other two. A great number of meetings result and everybody grows to appreciate and love the problem; in fact it becomes the *raison d'être* for some – their jobs depend on it and no conclusion is ever reached.

The board of directors – executive or not

Boards of directors of companies which are limited under the Companies Acts have legal responsibilities and powers, but their meetings may cover many other aspects of the company's affairs. Over the last forty years there has been a trend towards change in the power structure which is worth noting. The board is appointed by the shareholders, and traditionally only one or two directors were executive officers of the company – usually the managing director and the deputy managing director; the chairman of the board and most of the other directors had no job inside the organization. Many organization structures had a two-layer appearance:

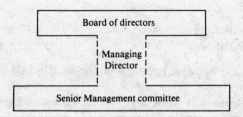

The board of directors met to consider broad strategy, policy and legal matters; the senior management committee met to consider everything else. In recent years this division of function has become less and less pronounced; indeed, in many companies the board of directors consists mainly of full-time executives. The distinction between responsibilities is no longer seen; it is now understood that senior management are better placed to formulate strategy and policy, as well as to ensure its execution. However, there is still a very important role for non-executive directors. As well as being shareholders' representatives, these people are objective and impartial. Often they have many other business interests, a factor which enables them to appraise proposals more keenly than the manager who lives with them from day to day.

Individuals v. committees

Of all the managerial activities discussed in this book, some are best handled by individuals acting on their own and others by committees. Research into executives' preferences has come up with the following suggestions:
Committee action is better for:

- Settling objectives
- Settling disputes
- Evaluating environmental change

Individual action is thought to be better from the viewpoints of:

- Leadership
- Getting things organized
- Planning
- Control
- Decision-making
- Communications

There are no apparent merits either way when it comes to innovation.

I must stress that these are only opinions and there is often room for an alternative approach. However, the consensus clearly indicates that individual action is more effective than group action.

If a meeting is suggested, ask:

■ Is it really necessary?
■ How can it be used to save time, money and effort?
■ How can it be managed so as not to waste time?

Finally, remember Parkinson's Law of Triviality* which states:
'. . . the time spent on any item of the agenda will be in inverse proportion to the sum involved.'

* *Parkinson's Law*, p. 69.

This chapter is concerned with the questions of why it is important to be able to communicate effectively and how this can be achieved.

Imagine that you are standing in the car park of a busy airport, but you cannot find the way into the terminal building. You see a man standing by a car, so you go up to him and ask him to direct you to the terminal. He does not reply, but merely stares at you. There are many possible reasons why the question which you put directly to him was not answered; for example:

- A plane took off at that moment and drowned your words.
- He could have been deaf.
- You could have been speaking in a foreign language (or had a strange accent) which he did not understand.
- You could have used a form of address that insulted or irritated him (e.g. ''Ere, you, where's the way in?').
- You might have been wearing a funny hat or strange clothing, or been carrying something which distracted his attention from what you were saying.

What went wrong?

In effect, what happened was that you – the sender of the message, the transmitter – failed to communicate with the man, the receiver of the message. This failure to communicate could have been caused by a number of factors, singularly or in combination:

- an interruption (the aircraft);
- a physical barrier (deafness);
- the wrong language;

- the wrong tone of voice;
- a distraction (funny hat).

Suppose the message does get across and the man hears you. He may decide that he is not interested in your problem (he has some of his own), so he walks away. Or he may point you in a certain direction and you go that way, only to find yourself in the aircraft maintenance hangar instead of the terminal building. If this happens, there are only three possible causes:

- he misled you (deliberately or not);
- he misunderstood you;
- you misunderstood him (or failed to follow his instructions).

In the situation I have described, we have to ensure that all the conditions are right, so that our chances of getting the message across are high. Moreover, it is not just a question of making sure that the receiver hears, but that he understands what he is hearing, and also that he is prepared to respond positively to what he hears.

In that scene at the airport we identified nine possible areas of difficulty which could have caused you to fail to get what you wanted. Some of the problems were connected with hearing the message, some with understanding it and others with responding positively to it. It was a simple communications issue with nothing very important at stake, so the failure did not result in great loss. But suppose that the communication had been a transatlantic telephone call in connection with a multi-million-pound sale of aero-engines. Had there been a failure of communications in such a conversation, someone could have lost a great deal of money – or finished up with many more engines than he needed.

There can be no doubt that there is not only a growing need to communicate more, but also a great need to ensure that communications are far more effective than they have been in the past. There is evidence that many organizational problems have been caused – or aggravated – by inadequate communications; managerial responsibility in this cannot be avoided.

The importance of effective communications

Communication is all about passing on information. It is either a request for information – 'Please send me your price list' – or the actual giving-out of information: 'Here is our price list.' There are many reasons why people give out or request information, and therein lies the importance of being effective with it. Information is required for all the aspects of organizational life which have been considered in this book: to help in planning, for better decision-making and problem-solving, for creating understanding between people and for effective control. Communication is needed not only to promote understanding but also to persuade: advertising is information communicated to potential customers in such a way as to persuade them to buy; public relations is information presented to the world in such a way as to persuade it that the organization is beneficial.

We could say that there is communication which is made for reasons of operational effectiveness, and communication made for political reasons (using the word 'politics' in its widest sense).

Most of an organization's communications effort is directed within the organization itself and is never seen outside. However, there is a fairly high proportion which concerns groups external to the organization and it is useful to consider these two aspects separately, looking at each from the viewpoint of the various receivers.

Internal communications

Inside an organization, you as a manager will have to communicate with several different types of people: your boss, your colleagues and your subordinates being the most common. In addition, if your organization is unionized you may have to devote a considerable amount of time to communicating with the union representatives. In all cases, by far the greater proportion of the communicating will be of the operational type – concerned with planning, doing the job and with control; but every manager has some political communications needs too – persuading the boss to decide an issue in a certain way, trying to introduce change to an old-fashioned work-force, negotiating for additional equipment with the accounts department. All these are political reasons for communicating, and to be a successful manager you will cultivate your talents in this direction, as well as using your operational communicative skills.

The manager and his boss

Sometimes one hears the statement: 'The trouble with my boss is, he never listens.' Why does a complaint like this arise?

On the assumption that there are no obvious physical barriers to communicating with the boss (the first two causes on p. 118), it must be the case that he is hearing, but is either not understanding or not responding for some other reason.

A lack of understanding can be caused by the wrong language (even though it may technically be right) or the wrong tone. So ask: Does he understand what he is being told? If the answer is, Yes, he does, but he still will not do anything, then you will have to find the reason for the lack of response. It could be that he is not interested, or that he thinks the problem can be solved without his interference.

It is part of every manager's job to learn to manage his boss. Being able to communicate with him is part of this, therefore the first step is to identify the cause of any problem. This, as we saw with problem-solving, can lead straight to the solution.

The manager and his subordinates

Every good manager must ensure that his subordinates have the opportunity to communicate with him regularly, not only by having an open-door policy – 'Come in and see me at any time' – but also by taking the trouble to actually be available in their place of work frequently. If this is done irregularly it will be considerably less effective, because it is only with constant appearances that a level of familiarity is built up so that people are willing to talk freely. It is not uncommon for young office workers to literally tremble at the thought of being spoken to by a senior manager whom they rarely see.

To establish a degree of goodwill and trust between yourself and subordinates will help you – as a manager – to find out more about attitudes and atmosphere than a whole shelf of statistical reports, and will also enable you to approach the change process on a more relaxed, participatory basis.

In return for a flow of information upwards, staff expect information to be passed downwards too. The expression, 'the information filters down', is not a good commendation for an organization's skill at communicating. One of the causes of concern felt by trade unions nowadays is the issue of disclosure of information. They feel that the ordinary working individual, particularly in a large organization, is being kept in the dark over too many issues, particularly those at the corporate strategy and policy level.

Research has indicated that a few companies have deliberate policies to restrict the amount of information given out to employees, but many avoid disclosing information only if it is 'sensitive' – in other words it would be harmful to the organization if a competitor heard something too soon. Possibly the majority of organizations simply do not consider the question to be important. However, there is a growing trend for the increased dissemination of information and this is noticeable amongst the more progressive companies. The staff newspaper or magazine has long been a feature of corporate attempts at communication. Nowadays specially designed reports are being prepared alongside annual reports and accounts, in order to explain the significance of the firm's profit and loss account and balance sheet information.

All these efforts do not mean that you as manager can give up worrying about the question. On the contrary, your responsibility is to explain the significance of these formal communications and to inform your staff about developments and changes taking place in your own department.

The manager and the trade union

Apart from the regular communications which take place between managers and trade union representatives, many managers find that a good deal of time and effort needs to be spent –

whether in or out of meetings – in negotiating and bargaining with the union representatives. It has been said that the existence of strong works councils in such countries as Germany, Sweden and Norway is a major factor in accounting for their low industrial dispute statistics. The purpose of the works council is seen as an effective vehicle for good communications – both of information (to create understanding) and of persuasion (to avoid conflict).

The manager and his colleagues

It appears that managers generally spend as much time with their colleagues as with their subordinates or bosses. This partly reflects the nature of the problems that managers face and partly the trend towards delegated responsibility, as we saw in the case of the matrix organization. Good communication with your peers is important where problems need to be solved together, where each of you is facing a similar problem or where the formal channels of communication (i.e. up and down the line) are slow, inefficient or politically inappropriate.

For example, if a factory manager finds that he is in danger of running out of a particular component, he is in a good position to avoid a crisis if he can phone the appropriate purchasing manager and request more. If he does not know or has never met his counterpart, then there may be a communications barrier which in an emergency will cause trouble.

External communications

An organization and its managers have to be in constant communication with many different groups of people. Some managers have considerable responsibility in this respect, whereas others have only limited contact with the outside world.

Any list of external contacts will include:

Banks	Local press/radio
Customers	The law
Employment bureaux	National Insurance officers
Factory inspectorate	National newspapers/TV

Finance houses/insurance companies	Pressure groups
Gas/electricity/water boards	Shareholders
Government and politicians	Suppliers
Other government departments	Taxman
Local authority	Trade unions
The local community	VAT man

Some of the communications activities are strictly commercial, such as selling and buying; others are purely financial or legal. All these are handled by experts in the appropriate skills and professions, whose ability to communicate effectively is closely related to their professional skills. The skilled salesman communicates with prospective customers better than the company's doctor (at least we hope he does) because his training and experience have taught him how to be effective in this sphere. Similarly, the accountant's skill at communicating with the tax authorities is a result of his training.

However, there are other very important aspects of external communications which need to be mentioned.

Political role   Some of the communications which takes place between an organization and its environment is designed to show a group, or groups, of people that the organization is an acceptable, creditable institution in society. This is the political role of the organization and is an important part of the work of managing directors and other senior managers. To ignore this activity is possibly to fail to build bridges of confidence with various power groups in society as a whole.

Information   Every organization must receive information from the environment, other than from its obvious commercial sources such as its customers and suppliers. This is the information that is needed for assessing threats and opportunities. To have an effective radar system, an organization must have good listeners and watchers. This kind of activity is all too often left to chance and casual encounter.

In all communications situations (both internally and externally) if you are intending to send a message and you want a positive response, you must always ask these three questions:

- With whom do I wish to communicate (the audience)?
- What do I wish to communicate (the message)?
- How do I communicate (the method)?

The audience

Determining precisely who makes up the audience may sound easy and often it is. If I wish to speak to the bus conductor, I know precisely who my audience will be. But suppose I want to advertise soap – who is my audience then? (A little brainstorming here will produce some amusing answers.)

A second question to ask is: Is there anything about my audience that could prevent them from hearing or understanding what I am about to say? Just as with the man at the airport, there are several potential blockages and it is important to be able to identify these and avoid or overcome them. So the answer to this question will actually determine what we say and how we say it.

The message

In casual conversation, people adjust their language to suit their audience quite spontaneously and without thinking about it. In a working environment, however, a conscious effort has to be made to choose words and phrases carefully, so as to ensure that the message is received and understood. There are three main ways in which a poor choice of words can cause a communications problem:

1 Corporate jargon

All organizations develop their own jargon, sometimes to such an extent that it sounds almost like another language. People are referred to by their initials, documents are referred to by their code numbers, and the names of departments are abbreviated. This may be nice and convenient for the initiated, but to an outsider it is totally meaningless. Moreover, it also makes life exceedingly difficult for newcomers in the organization; indeed, a useful addition to an induction programme would be a corporate language dictionary.

2 Professional and technical jargon

A similar specialized use of words is to be found wherever experts in a particular area get together. These special languages are incomprehensible to outsiders, but are quite common; doctors have one, accountants have another, so do motor mechanics, plumbers and stockbrokers. If you know and use a technical language, you should take great care to ensure that the person you are addressing is a member of your 'jargon club'.

3 Multiple meanings

A great deal of misunderstanding occurs in oral communications because a word that is used by one person to mean one thing is taken by someone else to mean something quite different; e.g. there are many different meanings for the word 'stock', including:

Breeding source	Part of a rifle
Contents of store	Share in a company
Fill up	Store
Flower	Soup

If we take the plural 'stocks', we can add many more meanings. The problem would be compounded if a British and an American businessman were in conversation, because stock to the American would be the shares in a company, whereas common British business usage has stock to mean the contents of the stores or warehouse.

So as far as the message is concerned, try to choose words which the listener will not confuse with others and which he will understand. Use his language, not your own.

The method

If you wanted to tell a group of salesmen about a new product, you could write to them all, phone them all, interview each individually or call them together for a meeting. The most efficient way of getting the message across is to call a meeting of all the salesmen; it has these points in its favour:

- the salesmen will both hear about the product and see it;
- there will be an opportunity to ask and answer questions;
- it is less time-consuming than an individual approach;
- you can guarantee that everyone who should get the message actually receives it;
- it gives the salesmen a chance to meet each other and discuss common problems, and helps to improve motivation.

The other methods of communicating are not necessarily wrong; it is just that the sales conference is probably the best way of getting the message across in this case – even though it may well be more expensive than a letter or a series of individual interviews.

There are many different ways to answer the question: How do I get the message across? Messages can be spoken or written; come in pictures, in sound or in signs. They can be directed at the receiver's eyes, ears or even the other senses. They may be conducted by an individual using his own skills alone, or they may involve the use of technology such as radio and electronic systems. The choice has to be made with care, always bearing in mind the further question: Which has the best chance of success? We need to look at some of the main communicating methods in terms of their overall suitability, limitations and potential dangers.

Face-to-face communication

It is recognized that the most powerful way of communicating can be the face-to-face method, where the listener sees and hears the person sending the message. This can range from a simple interview between a manager and his boss to the company management conference where the managing director may be addressing several hundred managers. Unfortunately many people are not good at verbal communication, and the potential power of the method is lost (possibly even having the opposite effect to that desired).

Some ways of being boring

- Speak about a boring subject.
- Talk at length.
- Use long words and sentences, with a lot of technical jargon.
- Speak in a monotone.
- Speak in the first person: 'I did this, I did that.'
- Avoid humour.
- Try to be pompous.

In addition, if you want to make your audience a bit hostile, tell them that they are wrong, you are right; that they know nothing and you know everything!

Some ways of rousing interest and getting support

- Plan very carefully what you intend to do.
- 'Stand up; speak up; shut up.'
- Do the opposite of the things listed in the 'how-to-be-boring' section.
- Use visual aids if appropriate: pictures, models, a list of key words on a screen, a display of the key numbers.
- Practise.

Written reports

Written reports are valuable where face-to-face contact is impossible, or where the information needs to be studied and given a lot of thought. However, a poor report quickly becomes a dust-gathering pile of waste paper.

In the last chapter we noted that a great deal of time can be wasted if reports are exceedingly long. Moreover, many reports are badly written and the problem of wasted time is therefore compounded, because effort has to be spent 'translating' into a language that can be understood.

A report may be simply an account of what has been going on inside a part of an organization. It may be a document describing a piece of research – a fact-finding survey, for example; or it may present the findings of a problem-solving team, e.g. 'Recommendations for changing the system of bonus payments.'

Brevity is always welcome, especially for narrative reports which simply relate that everything has gone according to plan. Keep these as brief as possible.

With all reports, busy managers want to see the conclusions; make sure these can be easily found and understood. In writing a report – or for that matter a simple memo – be sure to answer the following questions at the outset:

- Who wants it?
- What precisely do they want?
- Why do they want it?

If the answers to these questions are not clear, then no further work should be carried out until they have been answered properly. Thereafter the job is largely one of gathering the facts – background data, specific information on the matter in question, case histories if necessary, interviews and so on. All this information has to be sifted and sorted, leaving out everything irrelevant. The reader should have all the information he needs, and none that is unnecessary.

Having done this, the next stage is to design the report itself. Here it is worth bearing in mind the contents of the following note, which Winston Churchill sent to government departments when he was Prime Minister:

To do our work, we all have to read a mass of papers. Nearly all of them are far too long. This wastes time, while energy has to be spent in looking for the essential points.

I ask my colleagues and their staffs to see to it that their reports are shorter.

  i The aim should be reports which set out the main points in a series of short, crisp paragraphs.

  ii If a report relies on detailed analysis of some complicated factors, or statistics, these should be set out in an appendix.

  iii Often the occasion is best met by submitting not a full-dress report, but an *aide-mémoire* consisting of headings only, which can be expanded orally if needed.

  iv Let us have an end of such phrases as these: 'It is also of importance to bear in mind the following considerations . . .', or 'Consideration should be given to the possibility of carrying into effect . . .' Most of these woolly phrases are mere padding, which can be left out altogether, or replaced by a single word. Let us not shrink from using the short expressive phrase, even if it is conversational.

Reports drawn up on the lines I propose may at first seem rough as compared with the flat surface of officialese jargon, but the saving in time will be great, while the discipline of setting out the real points concisely will prove an aid to clearer thinking.

W. S. C.
10 Downing Street

Other points on report writing

- Each section should be numbered (see any official government report).
- Break up a long report with simple charts and diagrams.
- Avoid slang or foreign expressions.
- State the precise source of quotations.
- Avoid generalizations unless supported by facts (e.g. 'all multinationals are immoral' is not a valid statement, but 'Multinationals can wield considerable financial power' is valid).
- Watch the 'fog index', which is a measure of how obscure a piece of writing can be. The longer the sentence and the longer the words in the sentence, the foggier the communication.

Signs and signals

Signs and signals are much more common than you may think. There are signals which people make to each other: deliberate ones such as a nudge or a wink, and unconscious ones such as body language, whereby our gestures signify things that our speech may be hiding.

However, most signs are written or painted and are created to inform us of something. They are found everywhere and sometimes they fail because the receiver does not know how to interpret them.

There is a little sign on the cover of this book; now that you know it, you will recognize it if you see it again as the Pan 'logo'. Every day you will see signs you do not recognize, because the creator has failed to make it clear what the sign represents. However, when we do tell people the meaning, we have a powerful communicating device at our disposal.

In organizations, signs and symbols are frequently used as an integral part of the control system, to draw the attention of key people to those things which need it. This may range from a piece of information being underlined or circled, to a series of flashing lights on the control panel of a machine.

Pictures and diagrams

When they are well-presented, pictures and diagrams are a great help in making good communications; poor pictures are a waste of time, money and effort. To be effective they should be:

- clear;
- simple;
- relevant;
- well-made.

Numbers

In the next chapter I will be looking at the use of numbers in more detail, but the general rules already mentioned should be noted: keep them simple, and few. If you have to show details, put these in appendices or supporting papers.

Technological help

Technology helps the communications process in a great many ways. You will find the following pieces of technology in any office: a pen, a telephone, a typewriter. In addition, in nearly every home there is a radio and a television set. Every day, most people see a newspaper, a magazine or a book, and many receive correspondence through the letter-box which has been sorted by a machine. Many homes now have tape recorders and some have televisions which can be linked to the Post Office computer via the Prestel system.

At the office, many managers now have small television-like screens on their desks. These visual display units (VDUs) can provide each manager with up-to-date information about the items under his control. (VDUs can also be seen at the check-in desks at airports.) Computers are now available in all shapes, sizes and prices, and they all process information.

All this is communications technology. Many of the items listed above can be powerful ways of communicating because, as in the case of newspapers or TV, they reach millions of people. Some are designed to quickly process huge amounts of data, others are there to help individuals to be better managers.

Many people believe that the next 10–20 years will see a huge surge in the growth of electronic information systems. Most of the necessary technological know-how exists already; it is a matter of cost and of hard work in assembling it. For instance, it is now possible to turn written words into a kind of speech; information is fed in by a tape or punchcard, and through a speaker comes a sort of 'voice'. However, the other way around is difficult – to get the human voice turned into writing. Nevertheless this is a real possibility for the near future and its appearance will have many uses. A manager will be able to talk to a computer and ask for information which now has to pass through several time-consuming stages.

Technology will therefore:

- speed communications;
- save time;
- bypass the need to travel;
- provide more and better information, very fast.

Nevertheless, its success will depend on the skill of the person sending the information in the first place (or the individual's ability to ask the right question) and also on how the data is interpreted.

Listening

Most of this chapter has been concerned with the sending side of communications, but it is important never to forget that listening is just as vital. Without effective listening, there can be no effective communication.

It has been discovered that people forget most of what they have heard within a couple of days. This can be improved by better messages, repeated messages and also by helping the receiver to learn to be a more efficient listener. Among the many ideas for better listening are:

- Concentrate on what is being said, not on who is saying it.
- If you do not understand, ask for a repeat, if you can.
- Try to concentrate on the meaning of the message (ignore distractions; avoid daydreaming).
- Do not become emotionally involved (it is very easy to be roused to anger or another emotion and thus miss a key point).
- Remember that thoughts are quicker than words and you can evaluate what is being said without missing anything.
- Do not take many notes – just the key points – and (if important) write them out fully after the speaker has finished.

Feedback

As we have seen, communication is not merely about passing on messages, but is concerned with understanding, persuading and learning. If we have been communicating to others and we want to find out whether the message was received, understood and will be acted upon, it is vital to get feedback. In other words, we must make sure that the receiver of the message communicates back to us; we must assume nothing.

Equally, if we are receiving the message, then we have a responsibility to give feedback to the sender (where the message is for us). This is particularly true for managers who have frequent communications with their subordinates. Let them know what you think they have said; test your understanding of the message. In that way, better communication will result.

All managers have to use numbers from time to time and their use is on the increase. Some managers probably feel that the numbers are a nuisance and hinder good management. However, properly used, there is no doubt that they can be very helpful and all managers need to be able to work comfortably with them.

Here is a simple example of the need to be able to work with numbers:

Suppose you ran a shoe-shop. Each week you have to order shoes from the warehouse; how do you decide on the quantity to order? You might:

- make a guess,
- stick a pin in a list of numbers.
- order the same as last week's order.
- order the same number as was sold last week,
- look at the trend over a few weeks and order more or less than last week accordingly.

It is most likely that you would use the last method because you would want to see if the demand for each type was rising or falling. If demand was going up, you would probably order more than the week before. If demand had been falling, you would estimate the number of shoes that would be sold and place an order to cover likely demand, bearing in mind the number already in stock.

Consider the following example, which shows the sales of a particular style of shoe over a five-week period, and also the number of pairs of shoes ordered:

Week number	1	2	3	4	5	6
Number of pairs of shoes in stock at the beginning of the week:	0	3	4	3	3	3
Number of pairs of shoes delivered on Monday mornings:	10	10	10	13	15	
Number of pairs of shoes sold each week:	7	9	11	13	15	
Number of pairs of shoes left on Saturday night:	3	4	3	3	3	

The question is: How many pairs of shoes should be ordered for delivery on Monday morning of week 6? The answer depends on the answer to yet another question, namely: How many pairs of shoes do we think will be sold?

If we look at the trend, it is easy to see that over the five weeks, the number of shoes sold has risen by two pairs each week. Therefore if fifteen pairs were sold last week, we might expect seventeen pairs to be sold this week. We cannot, of course, be certain about this, but the trend suggests seventeen, so if we begin with this number, the next steps are easy:

- we have in the store three pairs;
- we will sell about seventeen pairs; therefore
- we need to order fourteen pairs for delivery on Monday morning.

If all this happens, at the end of the week we will have no shoes of this type left on the shelves. However, to be safe – in case customers come flooding in – we ought to have a few pairs in reserve and so we need to order some extra. How many more than the fourteen pairs? There is a fair chance of selling fifteen pairs in total; some chance of selling sixteen; a small possibility of seventeen. So order seventeen pairs; after all if they are not sold, next week's order can be reduced.

This is a simple example of the use of numbers in planning and decision-making. Unfortunately, many small firms fail to make the most of their opportunities because they do not spend enough time studying the numbers and going through the kind of analysis described above. Indeed, many small businesses do not even collect enough numbers to help them to get better decisions and control more effectively; they simply collect the minimum required by law.

In the next few pages some of the ways of coming to terms with numbers are explained, so that they can be handled confidently. Some techniques which can help managers be more effective are also introduced.

How to handle big numbers

In the example above, the numbers being used were very small and probably caused no problem, but suppose the numbers we had been using had been much bigger? Would it have been any more difficult to arrive at a decision if we had been discussing gallons of oil to a petrol station? Or gallons of petrol to the oil refineries?

The biggest company in the world in terms of sales (General Motors) has a sales turnover in excess of $100,000,000,000. It is not easy to comprehend such vast numbers when they are written out in that way, but if we talk about $100 billion it does not seem quite so formidable.

The fact is that numbers are all relative in size. To speak about 'big' or 'small' alone is irrelevant; what matters is the size of the number in relation to other numbers with which it can be compared. So that we may compare General Motors with Ford and discover that Ford has sales of only (!) $63 billion. Moreover, we may also discover that General Motors' sales were $96 billion in the previous year.

Hence the first rule in dealing with big numbers is:

■ Do not be put off if the number seems particularly large. Many people eliminate all but the first three or four digits from the left so as to make it easy to add up and compare: so that General Motor's sales becomes $100 billion, the distance from London to Chicago is about 4,000 miles and the population of Great Britain is about 54 million. This is the rounding-off technique; it is only necessary to count to the last penny if you are a banker, an accountant or a cashier actually handling cash. In planning, decision-making and in control it is often unnecessary to go into the finest detail.

The second rule about numbers is:

■ Do not look at numbers in isolation; compare them with others. Only by comparing can you begin to draw any conclusions about a number and it often helps if the numbers can be converted into ratios such as percentages.

The numbers game reviewed

It is possible to consider the functions of management as threefold:

■ Planning
■ Actions
■ Control

and within each function numbers are used extensively.

Numbers in planning

These are used in the following ways:

■ To collect information about trends in the environment. This involves the technique of forecasting – looking ahead to see what you think is going to happen.
■ To assess the present position of the organization and its strengths and weaknesses. This involves the technique of appraisal.
■ To calculate where the organization will be if the present strategies, policies and activities continue; another forecasting requirement.
■ To help evaluate proposed alternative courses of action. This is the stage in planning where a number of strategies or options are available. Numbers can sometimes help to eliminate the poor alternatives – and even point to the best.

Moreover, some questions have to use numbers: how much to raise prices (or taxes or rates); whether to invest in certain projects; how much to borrow and so on.
■ To quantify the organization's plans – the creation of budgets and standards, after the decisions have been made as a result of the previous point.

Numbers related to actions

Every action inside an organization creates a number. Many of these numbers have to be recorded properly especially those which involve money. For limited companies, there is the legal requirement to keep records. In addition, tax people and the VAT inspectors need to see properly kept books of account, as they are termed (if these are unavailable, it is easy to pay too much tax).

Traditionally, keeping proper records of transactions involving money was for four purposes:

■ to prevent fraud;
■ to detect fraud (if it happened);
■ to work out the amount of profit on a deal;
■ to decide how to share out profits.

All these are still valid reasons for keeping proper records, but nowadays many records are also kept purely for the benefit of the managers – information to help them manage more effectively. Some of it is related to money and profits, but some is purely statistical: details of volumes and quantities made or sold; hours worked; employees hired; numbers of lorries and cars and so on.

Managers need most of these numbers, but there is a danger – especially with computer-based information systems – of producing too much information and drowning the unfortunate manager in a sea of numbers.

Numbers for control

We saw in Chapter 2 how control systems work; they are the joining together of planned numbers and actual numbers. The joining process produces variances, and you will remember that the really important thing about information in this area is the need to identify significant variances. Associated with this was the idea of reporting only the exceptional variances. Therefore, the third rule in handling numbers is:

- Wherever possible simplify, by eliminating all but those figures which are really important.

The principles set out in the last chapter in relation to communications generally are important here. If detailed statistics are likely to be needed, show these in an appendix or in supplementary papers.

How to handle a complicated page of numbers

- Ask if it really is anything to do with you, i.e. How does it help?
- Ask someone (preferably the creator) to explain it.
- Identify key words, especially 'total', 'forecast', 'actual', 'estimate'.
- Underline, in bright colours if you can, key numbers, especially totals and significant variances. (Circle adverse variances in red, favourable ones in green.)
- Transfer the important data on to another piece of paper, simplifying as you go (getting rid of the pennies and rounding off).
- If the table is a list of numbers, it is a good idea to look at the middle number (this is usually called the 'median'), and the numbers a quarter of the way down (from the top) and a quarter of the way up (from the bottom). These are known as the upper and lower quartiles.

To calculate the extremes in a range of results, ignore the top and the bottom result – they could be exceptional for many reasons. Use instead the results two, three or four places away from the extreme ends (depending on the size of the list). For example, in a list of all the numbers from 1 to 23, 12 is the median, the quartiles are 6 and 18, and 2 and 22 represent the range.

What is average?

Here is a list of the times taken by different trains to cover the journey from London to Preston.

HOURS AND MINUTES

2.31	2.39	3.01	4.02
2.32	2.47	3.03	
2.38	2.50	3.05	
2.39	2.58	3.16	
2.39	3.00	3.18	
2.39	3.00	3.49	

The list has been arranged in order of speed and the numbers have been split up into groups of three. These are simple devices for making reading and calculating easier. Most people would calculate the average journey time like this:

- Add together all the journey times in the list (this adds up to 3,386 minutes for the nineteen journeys)
- Divide the total number of minutes by the total number of journeys. This gives a figure of 178 minutes per journey, or 2 hours 58 minutes per journey.

This, we would say, is the average journey time. Technically it is known as the 'arithmetic mean' and is very useful for making comparisons between activities from bowling and batting in cricket to the efficiency of different salesmen, or the amount of money spent on books by different education authorities.

The arithmetic mean is not the only way of calculating an average, the other common one (there are several others) being the 'median', which we used earlier to find the middle of the range. These two measures of average usually work out almost the same; the choice depends on what you want to do with the average.

Using numbers in forecasting

The point has already been made that since the future is uncertain, forecasts are purely estimates and cannot be guaranteed. However, as we saw with the example of the shoe-shop at the beginning of the chapter, some attention to the numbers we have available helps to produce a more likely forecast than merely sticking a pin in a list of options.

At one end of the forecasting scale there is the shot-in-the-dark approach, and at the other a number of sophisticated techniques using computers which have been shown to produce better forecasts. Between them is the technique called 'extrapolation', which was used in the shoe-shop example.

Extrapolation involves looking at a trend and trying to calculate what will happen next. Estimates made by extrapolation can be obtained in several ways: drawing graphs is one of the simplest, and using various mathematical formulae is another. Extrapolation is widely used and can produce good forecasts.

The technique which is proving even more useful these days is 'regression analysis': an excellent example of modern scientific management at work, and particularly useful in sales and profit forecasting.

Regression is a mathematical exercise which involves relating a number of factors to whatever it is we are trying to forecast. A simple regression is where there is only one factor affecting the item being forecast. For example, if we say that sales of ice-cream are dependent on the temperature, we can calculate historically how closely the two move together. If there is more than one variable affecting sales, the term used is 'multiple regression'.

The problem with multiple regressions is that the greater the number of variables, the further back into history you have to go in order to get enough information to be able to test whether the variables really are relevant. The more information you have, the more involved the sums; to do the job properly, a computer is needed.

Moreover, it is necessary to get estimates of the variables that have been found to affect sales, costs or whatever it is we are forecasting. Often these are economic estimates, and various organizations specialize in making them, as we have seen.

Regression has to be used with care because it depends on the knowledge and understanding of the manager in identifying the important factors that affect his operations. No amount of sophisticated computer analysis can generate good forecasts if understanding of the environment is poor.

Using numbers in making decisions

Many decisions, especially in business, relate ultimately to money. They are concerned with costs, revenue or profit – or all three. Sometimes it is possible to calculate the alternatives with certainty, so that, for instance, if we buy coffee in one shop it will cost us £1.99; if we buy it in another, it will cost £2.08. The numbers provide the answer and the decision is easy. Unfortunately many decisions are taken under conditions of great doubt, where the outcome is uncertain. In business, the reason is often that predicting demand for products or services is not at all easy and this leads to dealing in probabilities – the chance of selling nothing, or a few, or many, or a million. In such circumstances the technique that can help is called 'decision analysis'.

The steps of decision analysis are as follows:

Step 1. List all the possible courses of action.

Step 2. List all the possible results (usually known as outcomes).

To take a simple example, Walter Bottle had £100,000 in the bank, earning 8% interest. One day he saw for sale a small country inn costing exactly £100,000, which would produce a guaranteed profit of exactly 20%.

Obviously, on purely financial grounds Walter would be better off putting his money into the inn. But suppose the result was guaranteed only if there was no competition: if someone built another inn nearby, Walter calculated that the profit would be nearer 5%. Now the course of action is not so obvious, because there is a possibility of being worse off by investing in the project. So:

Step 3. Set out the alternatives:

Actions / Events	Do nothing	Invest in the project
No competition	8% = £8K*	20% = £20K
Competition	8% = £8K	5% = £5K

This is sometimes called a 'payoff table', because it shows all the possible alternative results.

At this point either a decision can be taken, or more information can be obtained and calculations carried out. Therefore:

Step 4(a). Make a decision now, by choosing an action based on what you think is the most likely outcome; e.g. I think there will be no competition, therefore the best course of action is to invest in the project.

Another way of making the decision now would be to select the course of action which gives you the 'best-worst' outcome. This means that if the money is left in the bank, the worst possible outcome is 8%. Alternatively, if the money is invested in the project the worst possible outcome is 5%. The best-worst outcome is 8%, so the decision is: leave the money in the bank.

This method tries to avoid the worst possible results, but since it concentrates on the worst possible in all cases, it ignores the great potential that exists.

Step 4(b). Assess probabilities.

This is where personal judgement and skill enter into the picture, and the way of approaching this step is to follow these three rules:

- Each possible outcome should be given a probability number on a scale of 0 to 1.0.
- If it is impossible (if you think it cannot happen), give it a probability rating of 0.

* K is 'shorthand' for a thousand.

■ All the possible outcomes must add up to 1.0 (by definition, one must happen and after the event all the other possible outcomes are 0).

For example, in horse-racing the odds are another way of assessing the probability of a horse winning. If there are four horses, we could have a list like this:

Horse	Probability of winning	
A	0.3	
B	0.1	Total probabilities = 1.0
C	0.4	
D	0.2	

A dead-cert would theoretically have a probability of 1.0 and all the others 0.0!

In the investment decision example Walter decides that the probability of competition is 0.2. Therefore the chances of no competition are 0.8.

Step 5. Calculate the expected value of each outcome.

This simply means multiplying the probabilities by the appropriate outcomes in each case. Our payoff table can be expanded to show how this looks:

	Do nothing	Invest in project	Probability
No competition	£8K	£20K	0.8
Competition	£8K	£ 5K	0.2

The calculations to get the expected values are:

1 *Do nothing*

		Outcome	Probability		
No competition	=	£8,000	× · 0.8	=	£6,400
Competition	=	£8,000	× 0.2	=	£1,600
Expected value (EV)				=	£8,000

2 *Invest in project*

	Outcome		Probability		
No competition	= £20,000	×	0.8	=	£16,000
Competition	= £ 5,000	×	0.2	=	£ 1,000
Expected value (EV)				=	£17,000

The size of the expected values gives us a clue as to which course of action to take. The figures are not guaranteed, however, and Walter realized that:

■ the expected values were only as good as his probability estimates; and
■ he could still get the worst outcome. (He had to ask himself if he was still willing to accept the risk – could he afford the worst outcome?)

It is essential to remember these two points in all investment decision exercises.

Decision trees

A common way of presenting decision analysis is by way of a diagram. Using the example which has just been discussed, the diagram known as a 'decision tree' is illustrated below:

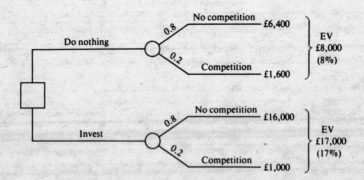

Other decision-making aids

A whole range of techniques similar to those already described is available to help managers to make better decisions. What they have in common is that they adopt mathematical techniques to help solve problems, but none of them can take the decision; that remains the manager's job.

Techniques such as linear programming, critical path analysis, and others in what is sometimes called 'operational research', are all decision-making aids at your disposal. Their use is made a great deal easier with computers – indeed, many are impossible without them.

Linear programming is particularly useful in production planning, where there are numerous products which can be made on many different machines with different costs and rates of production.

Critical path analysis is used on projects like buildings and ships, where a hold-up – such as waiting for a component or for a job to be finished – can cost a great deal of money.

In the financial world the technique called 'discounted cash flow' (DCF) is recognized as being an invaluable method for capital budgeting, i.e. for assessing the likely profitability of an investment over the life of that investment.

'Break-even analysis' is another useful financial technique that will help you to appreciate just what level of business has to be achieved before your firm makes any profit at all. This and the related technique of 'marginal costing' are helpful in calculating the effects of an increase or decrease in the price of a product or service – one of the businessman's most difficult, regular decisions.

Two important things to remember

Keep it simple

It is so easy to become involved in complicated mathematics simply because the techniques are available. Often a few quick, simple calculations will give the answer.

Do not let the system take over

There was once a firm which sold garden sheds. Every shed sold had £20 added to the cost price to allow for overheads and profit; this was based on estimated sales of 100 sheds a week. At the end of four weeks, they discovered they had sold only 360 sheds, so they recalculated the mark-up and added £25 to the price instead of £20 as before. This, they reckoned, would enable them to make the level of profit they had originally planned. Unfortunately sales continued to fall, and in the next four-week period they amounted to only 340 sheds. So they did the calculation again and increased the price once more. You can imagine what happened.

The point of this story is that the firm had allowed its system to take over. It was not an unreasonable way of fixing prices in the first place, but by reworking the numbers every four weeks they were digging a hole for themselves. There is a danger, for all organizations, of adopting techniques which become a normal part of operating practice and then regarding them as unchangeable. All systems must be reviewed constantly so as to ensure that they are still useful.

Scientific management

We introduced the idea of scientific management in Chapter 1 (p. 5) with the work of F. W. Taylor. Taylor was concerned with efficiency and with improving the way things were done. His conviction that there is a best way of doing things has become the basis of scientific management. Today the widespread availability of computers and calculators means that more and more information can be collected, stored and processed. This has helped to produce one of the great steps forward in management, namely the technique of model-building.

In the natural sciences, experiments are common and are often carried out in order to discover what happens if certain phenomena occur. If we pour water on a lighted match, the light goes out; if we pour petrol on it, we have an explosion. In management, like many social sciences such as psychology, the scope for experiment is limited. It is not possible for a company to change its prices every day until it finds the best price, partly because this is impractical, partly because of the huge range of prices that could be established, and partly because the economic conditions both outside and inside the firm change too fast for comparable measurement.

To overcome this, model-building is now growing in importance. Sometimes these may be physical models such as tiny bridges, ships or aircraft, but often they are built entirely of numbers or in code. In the same way, chess (and every other board-game) can be played without a board and pieces, just by using a specially built code.

Models are intended to help the manager understand better what is going on in the environment of the organization and what will happen if, inside it, he takes certain courses of action. A decision to drill for oil in the North Sea is such a problem – not wisely carried out on the back of an envelope, but requiring a long and painstaking analysis of many variables.

The first chapter opened up the world of the manager and we saw that this contains a great many elements. Towards the end of the chapter (p. 7) I made a list of all the different activities in which the successful manager must become involved, and have discussed many of these general managerial skills. Armed with this knowledge, therefore, it is now time to consider the attributes required of a successful manager in a little more detail, to find out what is important today and try to assess what will be important in the future.

Many lists of attributes have been drawn up in an attempt to describe the perfect manager. One such list is set out below:

Knowledge of
- their own area of specialization
- the organization
- the sector of the economy (or society)
- the environment of the organization
- management techniques and principles
- other areas of specialization that are relevant

Ability to
- solve problems ⎫
- take decisions ⎬ analytical skills
- relate to people ⎭
- build team spirit ⎫
- communicate ⎪
- persuade and negotiate ⎬ social skills
- delegate ⎪
- lead ⎭

Have personal qualities of
- emotional resilience (to cope with stress)
- creativity (some good ideas)

■ mental agility
■ positive thinking

These eighteen attributes of successful managers do not consti-
tute a comprehensive list. It is designed more to enable you to ask
the question: Do I know many managers who score highly in each
of these areas? It is quite likely that the great majority of managers
are strong in many areas but weaker in others; hence it is a useful
exercise to try out on yourself from time to time.

One attribute which was omitted from this list – and which we
should not forget – is that related to learning. The fact that very
few managers are likely to score ten-out-of-ten on all these
attributes suggests that some learning is needed in most cases.

No manager can afford to stop making a conscious effort to
learn, partly because no one's skills and knowledge can ever be
complete, even in a world that is standing still; partly because
knowledge is growing so fast, and partly because of the speed of
change.

The problem can be seen from the viewpoint of a manager who
wants to recruit someone to take over a top management job.
Whether in a school, a hospital, a bank or a manufacturing
concern, the problem is the same: namely, the attributes needed
to run the organization today are identifiable, but will they be the
same thirty years from now? To answer this, we need to refer to
some famous people in management and to see what they have
said about the features of a successful manager – in the past, now
and in the future.

Henri Fayol (again)

I have already discussed the five functions of management, but
there are two other aspects of the job, which were mentioned by
Fayol and which we must look at separately. They are his
'principles of management' and his ideas on the qualities and
training of managers.

Fayol identified fourteen principles, or guidelines, and he
emphasized that these are not rigid but have to be adapted to suit
the particular needs of the situation.

- Division of work – the need to specialize.
- Authority and responsibility – the manager's official status and his personal authority.
- Discipline – firm but fair.
- Unity of command – one boss to give the orders.
- Unity of direction – everyone pulling the same way.
- Subordination of individual interest to general interest – the group's needs come first.
- Remuneration – pay must be fair.
- Degree of centralization – the extent to which authority is or is not delegated.
- Chain of authority – must be maintained (unless it would cause harm to do so).
- Order – 'a place for everything and everything in its place', e.g. the organization chart and statements of areas of responsibility.
- Equity – kindliness and justice shown by managers help to produce loyalty from staff.
- Stability of tenure of staff – job security.
- Initiative – thinking out and acting on ideas, 'one of the keenest satisfactions of man'. Let subordinates exercise it.
- *Esprit de corps* – teamwork builds up the strength of an organization or a group.

Qualities needed in a manager

- physical: healthy, vigorous;
- mental: ability to understand and learn, judgement, mental vigour, adaptability;
- moral: firmness, acceptance of responsibility, initiative, loyalty, tact;
- general education: good general knowledge;
- special knowledge: for the work;
- experience.

Fayol also stressed the importance of managerial training – 'steady, methodical training of all employees and at all levels' – and made the point that a manager should not ignore his responsibility for his own training.

F. W. Taylor also had something to say about training:

It becomes the duty of those on the management side to deliberately study the character, nature and performance of each workman . . . The scientific selection of the workman and his development is not a single act; it goes on from year to year and is the subject of continual study on the part of management.

F. W. Taylor

F. W. Taylor's book *The Principles of Scientific Management* (published in 1911), was written for the following reasons:

First, to point out . . . the great loss which the country is suffering through inefficiency in almost all our daily acts.

   Second, to try to convince the reader that the remedy for this inefficiency lies in systematic management, rather than in searching for some unusual and extraordinary man.

   Third, to prove that the best management is a true science, resting upon clearly defined laws, rules and principles, as a foundation . . . and to convince the reader that whenever these principles are correctly applied, results must follow which are truly astounding.

Some more important views on the role of the manager

Blake's grid

Blake's grid is a common name for a technique called 'the managerial grid' which was developed by Dr Robert Blake and Dr Jane Mouton in the early 1960s. The grid's function is concerned with the development of organizations through the development of individual managers, and it is based on the idea that management has two concerns: the concern for people and the concern for production (although the word 'production' should not be taken literally, but signifies the job to be done). The grid itself is a simple chart, marked off in squares – see the diagram on page 154.

The numbers signify the extent of a manager's concern. Minimal concern is signified by number 1, and a very high level of concern by number 9.

All managers can be placed somewhere on the grid and five distinct basic styles can be identified from it:

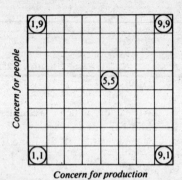

Concern for production

1,1. Signifies a style where minimum effort is put into getting the work done; just enough to keep the organization going.

9,1. Here the emphasis is on getting the job done and not paying much attention to human factors.

1,9. Here the primary concern is people, creating a good atmosphere and good conditions.

5,5. This is a balancing point – some concern for both factors.

9,9. In this extreme situation not only is the organization geared to satisfying the needs of people, but at the same time the job gets done. The aims and objectives of the individuals and the organization are very similar or – as the jargon puts it – there is a high degree of goal congruence (which means the same thing!).

Chester Barnard

One of the things which Chester Barnard said was that management needs a high degree of intelligence. He stated that to deal with all the many complications of business, considerable ability in logical reasoning and analysis is vital.

Remember, Barnard was writing in 1938. Since then organiz-ations have grown enormously in complexity as well as size. If it was a true statement in 1938, how much more important will it be in the year 2000?

Peter Drucker

No evaluation of the managerial task would be complete without reference to the contribution that Peter Drucker has made to the practice of management. In 1964 at the British Institute of Man-agement he made a speech which was called 'The Effective Executive', and in the course of it he made the following remarks:

It is amazing how great the differences are between one man in an executive position and another. There is not much difference in ability or intelligence, but one man gets things done and another never gets anything done . . . I believe that effectiveness is neither an ability nor a talent. It is a habit, a practice.

Drucker went on to discuss three things which all effective managers have in common:

- they understand the importance of managing time, especially in relation to decision-making;
- they accept responsibility for their own contribution, and for acquiring adequate knowledge, training and education in management, and 'whatever else one needs to know in the major disciplines and in their approaches to the job of building and running that terribly complicated institution, that terribly complicated structure, a modern business or any modern organization';
- effective people look for strength in others and build on it. Everybody has weaknesses and the manager's job is to neutralize them. The key question is: What can a man do?

More recently, Drucker has commented that the manager of tomorrow will have to do much the same things as today, but will have to tackle them with more knowledge and more thought. In addition there will be some changes, especially in the public services (hospitals, schools, government agencies etc.), where a more systematic approach to management will take place.

Two other areas of change will be in industrial relations and the social responsibility of organizations; in both cases, managers will have to take the lead and show much more concern.

The systems manager

The use of the word 'systematic' in the last-but-one paragraph is important because it is referring to a way of managing organizations which is becoming increasingly important: namely, the systems approach. The word 'system' has been used a number of times in this book, especially in relation to control and information.

The most appropriate way of explaining what is meant by 'systems' is to consider the way in which the parts of a living body can be described; such terms as the nervous system, the digestive system and the circulatory system are all familiar. They are the names given to essential functions of the body; the body being the total system. In the same way, organizations can be described as systems and contain many sub-systems on which the success of the whole depends.

However, unlike the human body, an organization's systems can be of any shape, size or form and can work in many different ways. Some are better developed than others; control systems are well understood and there is general agreement as to their essentials. However, many other systems are less well developed and completely absent in some cases. For example, it is believed that many organizations do not have any regular system for evaluating the environment – or even for analysing their own internal strengths and weaknesses.

The role of management can be described as making sure that there are sufficient systems within the organization to make it work, and that there systems are efficient so that the corporate body stays healthy. Essential ingredients in the development of good systems are good communications channels and information systems because, as in the human body, all the subsystems are linked to each other. If each does not know what is going on in the other parts, the whole body falls ill.

Some of the dangers of systems have already been highlighted: the silly system that helps nobody and hinders everyone; and the organization which is run for the benefit of the system. However, there is one other problem which needs to be emphasized – namely, that of inflexibility – and this is a problem that will grow as the rate of change accelerates. A great deal of effort is put into designing a major system within an organization, and the temptation is always there to preserve it, even though it may have outlived its usefulness. Flexibility in the design of systems is likely to be of considerable importance in the future, and to this end the coming of desk-top computers and similar devices is timely.

The futuristic manager

The following quotation comes from the book *The Management of Change*, which has already been quoted:*

The ratio of managers to workers will increase to handle the shift in the management orientation from the routine manipulation of material objects to the creation of ideas and the motivation of individuals to implement such ideas. Reflection and diagnosis will replace action as the prime activity of the manager.

The authors go on to state their belief that the successful manager of the future will have to encourage dissent, tolerate conflict and be willing to accept new ideas and new ways of working. Moreover, they consider that the team will have a much more important role in solving problems than it does today. In his most recent book, Alvin Toffler† considers that organizations of the future

* McGraw-Hill, 1974, p. 131.
† *The Adaptive Corporation*, Pan Books, 1985, p. 97.

will require people who can learn very fast – so as to be able to understand novel situations and problems – and have imagination – to as to be able to invent new solutions.

These views echo many of the ideas, theories and beliefs which have been quoted in this book. Some of them are debatable and indeed are being debated at length.

For example, a few year's ago Lord Weinstock wrote that the proper duty of industrial managers was to improve the efficiency of their own businesses, and that there was no single magic formula which would produce a 'stunning improvement' in British industry. He went on to stress the importance of training and of improving communications within companies.*

Finally, an article recently appeared on the management page of the *Financial Times*, entitled 'the Manager as a Paragon of All Virtues'.† The article reported the results of an exercise carried out by a team of leading European and American businessmen and academics to investigate 'management and management education in a world of changing expectations', under the joint auspices of the European Foundation for Management Development and the American Assembly of Collegiate Schools of Business. The picture that emerges of the manager of the future is that he will be a diplomat, a 'Renaissance man', a decision-maker, a negotiator, a persuader, a consensus-builder, a coordinator, and a strategic planner. These virtues will all be necessary because: 'While there will still be concern for the economic and technological factors, there will be much greater concern than in the past for the political, social and psychological impact of the organization.' The report also comments that the manager has traditionally been thought of as sitting in the centre of a circle, directing all the various activities of the organization from within it; but that today he sits on the periphery, dealing with the outside world while keeping an eye on what goes on inside the circle.

Whether or not you agree with these views is not as important as taking time out to decide which of all the ideas that have been given an airing in this book, you will have to develop in subordin-

* *Guardian*, 19 November 1980.
† 26 September 1980.

ates as well as in yourself. Perhaps this is best summed up by the late Lord Thomson of Fleet, who wrote in his autobiography* that if one wants to be successful, one must think until it hurts.

* *After I Was Sixty*, Hamish Hamilton.

Further Reading

Peter F. Drucker, *Management* (Pan Books, 1979)
Victor Vroom and Edward L. Deci, eds. *Management and Motivation* (Penguin, 1979)
John Adair, *Effective Decision Making* (Pan Books, 1985)
Penny Hackett, *Success in Management: Personnel* (John Murray, 1985)
Rosemary Stewart, *Managers and their Jobs* (Macmillan (new edition), 1986)
Barry T. Turner, *Effective Technical Writing and Speaking* (Business Books, 1974)
John Adair, *Effective Leadership* (Pan Books, 1983)
To keep up to date, read the following journals:
   Management Today and
   Harvard Business Review

Index

merit awards 46
Mintzberg, Henry 7
models 149
Montgomery, Lord 65
motivation 3, 5, 7, 50–67, 157
motivators 56–7
Mouton, Dr Jane 153
multi-skilling 62

Napoleon 65
needs 55
negotiating 7, 48, 150, 158
non-executive directors 115–16

objectives 10
organization structures 22–35
Osborn, Alex 110
Owen, Robert 52

paper, management of 102
Parkinson's Law 95
 law of triviality 117
participative management 59
pay and conditions 45–7
personnel planning 43–8
planning 4, 5, 7–17, 18, 21, 136,
 138–9, 158
planning horizon 9
policies 36–49
probability 144–6
problem-solving 6, 7, 68–80,
 108–9, 150
productivity 15, 37, 41, 62, 63
profit sharing 46
project planning 9, 17
publicity 39
public relations 39
purchasing 40–1

quality control 20–1
QWL (quality of working life) 62

quartiles 140

rational managers 79
recruitment of staff 43–5
redundancy, policy on 45
regression analysis 142–3
relationships, group 27–9
report writing 128–131
risk 16, 76, 146

scientific management 5, 148–9,
 153
secretaries 102–3, 114
self-actualization 55–6
self-respect 55
Simon, H. A. 79
span of control 24, 27–9
staff
 development and training 47–8
 dismissal 45
 redundancy 45
 selection 45
standards 18
Stewart, Rosemary 6–7
stock control 21
strategic planning 9, 14–16, 138,
 158
stress 87, 92
structure, organization 22–35
subordinates, number of 27–8
SWOT analysis 11
systems, control 20–21, 148,
 156–7

Tannenbaum and Schmidt 64
targets 10
Taylor, F. W. 5, 6, 64, 148, 153
teams 3, 53, 60–62, 66, 150, 157
technological change 13
technology in
 communications 131–3

Pan Management Guides

For busy executives who want to acquire quickly essential new management skills to develop their careers

Pan Management Guides will give today's hard-pressed executives and those who run their own businesses a more thorough grounding in essential management skills, sufficient to enable them to run their departments or businesses more effectively and successfully.

Pan Management Guides are written by authors who combine practical international experience of their subject with deep background knowledge. Each book in the series covers one crucial area of modern business so that a complete library of vital information can be built.

Pan Management Guides are down-to-earth and uncluttered, designed to enable you to quickly absorb only the facts that matter.

Books in the series:

Advertising and PR
Company Accounts
Essential Law
Financial Management
Industrial Relations
Management Accounting
The Management of Business
Marketing
Personnel Management
Production and Operations Management

Peter F. Drucker

The Practice of Management £4.95

'Peter Drucker has three outstanding gifts as a writer on business – acute
perception, brilliant skill as a reporter and unlimited self-confidence . . . his
penetrating accounts of the Ford Company . . . Sears Roebuck . . . IBM . . . are
worth a library of formal business histories' NEW STATESMAN

'Those who now manage ought to read it: those who try to teach management
ought to buy it' TIMES EDUCATIONAL SUPPLEMENT

Managing in Turbulent Times £2.95

This is Peter Drucker's latest and probably most searching analysis of the
problems and opportunities facing us as managers and individuals. This timely
and important book considers how to manage the fundamentals of business –
inflation, liquidity, productivity and profit – going on to demonstrate how
tomorrow's manager must concentrate his skills on managing innovation and
change – production sharing, new markets, redundancy planning, the
developing countries, transforming businesses to take account of changes in
the world economy.

Management £4.50

Peter Drucker's aim in this major book is 'to prepare today's and tomorrow's
managers for performance'. He presents his philosophy of management,
refined as a craft with specific skills: decision making, communication, control
and measurement, analysis – skills essential for effective and responsible
management in the late twentieth century.

'Crisp, often arresting . . . A host of stories and case histories from Sears
Roebuck, Marks and Spencer, IBM, Siemens, Mitsubishi and other modern
giants lend colour and credibility to the points he makes' ECONOMIST

All these books are available at your local bookshop or newsagent, or can be ordered direct from the publisher. Indicate the number of copies required and fill in the form below.

Send to: **CS Department, Pan Books Ltd., P.O. Box 40, Basingstoke, Hants. RG21 2YT.**

or phone: 0256 469551 (Ansaphone), quoting title, author and Credit Card number.

Please enclose a remittance* to the value of the cover price plus: 60p for the first book plus 30p per copy for each additional book ordered to a maximum charge of £2.40 to cover postage and packing.

*Payment may be made in sterling by UK personal cheque, postal order, sterling draft or international money order, made payable to Pan Books Ltd.

Alternatively by Barclaycard/Access:

Card No.

Signature:

Applicable only in the UK and Republic of Ireland.

While every effort is made to keep prices low, it is sometimes necessary to increase prices at short notice. Pan Books reserve the right to show on covers and charge new retail prices which may differ from those advertised in the text or elsewhere.

NAME AND ADDRESS IN BLOCK LETTERS PLEASE:

....

Name—————————————————————————————

Address————————————————————————————

—————————————————————————————————

—————————————————————————————————

3/87